Current
CONTROVERSIES

Teen Pregnancy
and Parenting

Other books in the Current Controversies series

Teen Pregnancy and Parenting

Lisa Frick, Book Editor

GREENHAVEN PRESS
An imprint of Thomson Gale, a part of The Thomson Corporation

Detroit • New York • San Francisco • New Haven, Conn. • Waterville, Maine • London

THOMSON

™

GALE

Christine Nasso, *Publisher*
Elizabeth Des Chenes, *Managing Editor*

© 2007 Thomson Gale, a part of The Thomson Corporation.

Thomson and Star logo are trademarks and Gale and Greenhaven Press are registered trademarks used herein under license.

For more information, contact:
Greenhaven Press
27500 Drake Rd.
Farmington Hills, MI 48331-3535
Or you can visit our Internet site at http://www.gale.com

LIBRARY OF CONGRESS CATALOGING-IN-PUBLICATION DATA

Teen pregnancy and parenting / Lisa Frick, book editor.
    p. cm. -- (Current controversies)
    Includes bibliographical references and index.
    ISBN-13: 978-0-7377-3295-5 (lib. hardcover : alk. paper)
    ISBN-10: 0-7377-3295-4 (lib. hardcover : alk. paper)
    ISBN-13: 978-0-7377-3296-2 (pbk. : alk. paper)
    ISBN-10: 0-7377-3296-2 (pbk. : alk. paper)
  1. Teenage pregnancy--United States. 2. Teenage mothers--United States.
3. Teenagers--United States--Sexual behavior. 4. Sex instruction--United States.
I. Frick, Lisa.
  HQ759.4.T43162 2007
  306.874'3--dc22

        2006020089

Printed in the United States of America
10 9 8 7 6 5 4 3 2 1

Contents

Chapter 1: Is Teen Pregnancy a Serious Problem?

Yes: Teen Pregnancy Is a Serious Problem

No: Teenage Pregnancy Is Not a Serious Problem

Many policy makers claim that teen pregnancy is a social burden because of the health risks involved and the poor life outcomes often experienced by mother and child. Recent studies, however, have found that some of the negative consequences have little to do with the mother's age.

Chapter 2: What Factors Contribute to Teen Pregnancy?

Chapter 3: Do Sex Education Programs Effectively Address Teen Pregnancy?

Sex education belongs in schools because most teens are too embarrassed to ask their parents about such matters. Teens deserve information on contraceptives, sexually transmitted diseases, and pregnancy so they can protect themselves.

No: Some Sex Education Programs Are Flawed

Chapter 4: Are Alternatives to Teen Parenting Good Options?

Chapter 5: Should Society View Teen Parenting Favorably?

Yes: Society Should View Teen Parenting Favorably

Through much of history, teen childbearing was viewed as normal because young people have lots of patience and energy. It is the way society has changed and postponed adulthood that makes teen pregnancy an issue today.

The stereotype of lazy, dependent, and irresponsible teen mothers does not hold true. While adolescent moms may need help in the short-term, they often push themselves to become independent, educated members of society.

No: Society Should Not View Teen Parenting Favorably

Some young mothers believe they are entitled to society's welfare and complain when they find the challenges of teen parenting difficult. This kind of social dependency is disturbing and should be condemned.

Even though many teen moms survive the challenges of parenting, their lives are filled with stress and financial worries and an inability to live a normal, teenaged life. Waiting to become a parent is a better alternative.

Foreword

By definition, controversies are "discussions of questions in which opposing opinions clash" (*Webster's Twentieth Century Dictionary Unabridged*). Few would deny that controversies are a pervasive part of the human condition and exist on virtually every level of human enterprise. Controversies transpire between individuals and among groups, within nations and between nations. Controversies supply the grist necessary for progress by providing challenges and challengers to the status quo. They also create atmospheres where strife and warfare can flourish. A world without controversies would be a peaceful world; but it also would be, by and large, static and prosaic.

The Series' Purpose

The purpose of the Current Controversies series is to explore many of the social, political, and economic controversies dominating the national and international scenes today. Titles selected for inclusion in the series are highly focused and specific. For example, from the larger category of criminal justice, Current Controversies deals with specific topics such as police brutality, gun control, white collar crime, and others. The debates in Current Controversies also are presented in a useful, timeless fashion. Articles and book excerpts included in each title are selected if they contribute valuable, long-range ideas to the overall debate. And wherever possible, current information is enhanced with historical documents and other relevant materials. Thus, while individual titles are current in focus, every effort is made to ensure that they will not become quickly outdated. Books in the Current Controversies series will remain important resources for librarians, teachers, and students for many years.

In addition to keeping the titles focused and specific, great care is taken in the editorial format of each book in the series. Book introductions and chapter prefaces are offered to provide background material for readers. Chapters are organized around several key questions that are answered with diverse opinions representing all points on the political spectrum. Materials in each chapter include opinions in which authors clearly disagree as well as alternative opinions in which authors may agree on a broader issue but disagree on the possible solutions. In this way, the content of each volume in Current Controversies mirrors the mosaic of opinions encountered in society. Readers will quickly realize that there are many viable answers to these complex issues. By questioning each author's conclusions, students and casual readers can begin to develop the critical thinking skills so important to evaluating opinionated material.

Current Controversies is also ideal for controlled research. Each anthology in the series is composed of primary sources taken from a wide gamut of informational categories including periodicals, newspapers, books, United States and foreign government documents, and the publications of private and public organizations. Readers will find factual support for reports, debates, and research papers covering all areas of important issues. In addition, an annotated table of contents, an index, a book and periodical bibliography, and a list of organizations to contact are included in each book to expedite further research.

Perhaps more than ever before in history, people are confronted with diverse and contradictory information. During the Persian Gulf War, for example, the public was not only treated to minute-to-minute coverage of the war, it was also inundated with critiques of the coverage and countless analyses of the factors motivating U.S. involvement. Being able to sort through the plethora of opinions accompanying today's major issues, and to draw one's own conclusions, can be a complicated and frustrating struggle. It is the editors' hope that Current Controversies will help readers with this struggle.

Introduction

Each year approximately nine hundred thousand U.S. teens become pregnant. Although the U.S. teen pregnancy rate has declined steadily since the 1990s, it remains the highest of any industrialized nation. While the rates have dropped, the rhetoric surrounding the issue has not. Policy makers, parents, politicians, and researchers continue to disagree about the impact and seriousness of teen pregnancy. Some contend teen pregnancy perpetuates many of society's leading problems, while others argue that teen pregnancy is just a symptom of those problems.

Whatever the case, behind the ever-contentious topic of teen pregnancy lies another issue—access to and information about contraceptives. While many sex education programs discuss how to use contraceptives, others do not. A majority of abstinence-only programs, which have seen increased federal backing in recent years, speak of contraceptives only in terms of failure rates.

Some studies have concluded that allowing access to contraceptives would reduce the teen pregnancy rate, but many policy makers are ideologically opposed. They believe allowing access to contraceptives inspires sexual behavior. In 2004 Wade F. Horn, the U.S. Department of Health and Human Services assistant secretary for children and families, testified before a Senate subcommittee discussing abstinence education. Horn said that he was worried about the double message some "abstinence-plus" programs provide, because they urge abstinence but also include information on contraceptives. "When you are talking with a child . . . who is not yet engaged in sexual activity, if you say, well, we would like you to not do it, but you know, just in case, let's give you a lot of instruction on how to use contraception, the real message that the young person gets is we don't expect you to actually embrace an abstinence goal but we really do expect that you are going to be sexually active."

The Alan Guttmacher Institute notes that while policy makers have said it is a priority to reduce unintended pregnancy, thirty-three states have recently enacted measures making it harder, and more expensive, for poor women and teenagers to gain access to contraceptives and related medical services. In an effort to determine the scope of influence that contraceptives have on unintended pregnancy, the Guttmacher Institute studied the matter and published its results in early 2006. Researchers rated each state for its efforts to reduce unintended pregnancy, taking into account services available, laws, policies, and public funding. California scored at the top of the list, followed by Alaska.

The study found that between 1992 and 2000 the states that made the greatest efforts to expand access to contraceptives also showed the highest drops in teen pregnancy. In California, for example, teen pregnancy dropped 39 percent. Alaska's rate dipped 34 percent. Yet in Nebraska, the lowest-ranking state in the survey, the teen pregnancy rate dropped just 17 percent in that period.

Guttmacher president Sharon L. Camp told the *Washington Post* that expanding access to reproductive services makes sense because every dollar spent on family planning saves three dollars in health care costs related to pregnancy. While some states have expanded access to contraceptives, others have sought to quell teen access through various legislative moves, mostly involving parental consent.

In Wisconsin, measures aimed at restricting teen access to contraceptives through the state's Healthy Women Program have been introduced more than once in recent years. According to the *Milwaukee Journal Sentinel*, supporters of the measure say that barring girls from receiving such services from the state would promote healthier sexual behavior among teenagers and would reestablish some parental rights.

"We have a situation where young girls are provided free birth control without parents' consent," state senator and bill supporter Glenn Grothman says. He argues that the availability of contraceptives encourages teen sex because it sends a message that adults do not really mind. Others feel the Healthy Women Program should not be altered because it helps cut down on teen pregnancy. One mother offered this rebuttal in the *Journal Sentinel*: "Teenage girls don't decide to have sex because they know birth control is available. In fact, most of them don't 'decide' in a rational manner at all. Some get carried away by their hormones; some are pressured by boyfriends . . . but I'm willing to bet that none of them has sex because they think adults approve."

Similarly, a measure called the Parents' Right to Know Act has been introduced in Congress a couple of times in recent years. It would require parental notification for contraceptives from federally funded health clinics. For many teenagers, particularly low-income teens, these clinics provide the only real means of obtaining prescription contraceptives. In 2002 the *Journal of the American Medical Association* reported that nearly 60 percent of sexually active girls under the age of eighteen would stop seeking reproductive health services if their parents had to be involved. Researchers in the study concluded that parental notification would, "impede girls' use of prescribed contraceptive services, with the majority of the girls continuing to have sexual intercourse despite restricted access to prescribed services."

Meanwhile, the debate rages on. While some argue that contraceptives are the best way to curb teen pregnancy, others believe an abstinence-only approach is best. The pros and cons of abstinence programs versus contraceptive training is one of the issues that authors discuss in *Current Controversies: Teen Pregnancy and Parenting*. They also examine whether teen pregnancy is a serious social problem, what factors contribute to teen pregnancy, if sex education programs effectively address teen pregnancy, if the alternatives to teen parenting are good options, and if society should look favorably on the continuing phenomenon of teen parenting.

Is Teen Pregnancy a Serious Problem?

Chapter Preface

Adolescent pregnancy occurs in all societies, yet its rate varies dramatically from country to country. In recent years researchers have focused their attention on the Netherlands, which boasts the world's lowest teen pregnancy rate. According to the Guttmacher Institute, a U.S.-based organization that seeks to protect and expand the reproductive choices available to all people, the Netherlands' teen pregnancy rate is roughly 12 pregnancies per 1,000 girls aged 15 to 19. The rate is nearly ten times higher—100 pregnancies per 1,000 young women—in the Russian Federation. Many Western European countries, including England and Scotland, have low rates—under 40 pregnancies per 1,000 young girls. Japan has similar numbers. Moderate rates (40 to 60 pregnancies per 1,000 girls aged 15 to 19) occur in Australia, New Zealand, and Canada. Only a handful of countries, including the United States, Romania, Belarus, Bulgaria, and the Russian Federation, have rates above 70 pregnancies per 1,000 young women. In the United States the rate stands at 84 pregnancies per 1,000 girls aged 15 to 19.

The wide variation in teen pregnancy rates puzzles both researchers and policy makers. In an effort to find an explanation for the variance, researchers Jane Lewis of England and Trudie Knijn of the Netherlands compared and contrasted the sex education programs of their countries. The results of their study, published in a 2002 issue of the *Journal of Social Policy*, found that many programs in England are subject to opposition and tend to change on the whims of politicians. The same can be said of programs in the United States. For example, in fiscal year 2005 President George W. Bush's budget requests included $186.4 million for abstinence education programs, which was a funding increase of $111.9 million over the previous year. In the Netherlands, however, politicians tend to steer clear of the topic, allowing professional sex educators to come to a consensus and formulate programs.

Lewis and Knijn also conclude that programs in England tend to focus on the negative aspects of sex and label it a risky behavior. A lot of the instruction focuses on how to say "no." The researchers noticed that the Dutch approach is different. They felt the Dutch accept that their teens will be sexually active, so instead of warning them of the dangers of sex, they try to introduce measures to deal with the consequences. In addition, the Dutch approach sex education nonchalantly, inserting it into "everyday living" courses and teaching it alongside bicycle repair and nutrition.

Looking for ways to improve his school's sex education program, principal Dave Harris of Nottinghamshire, England, traveled to the Netherlands for a firsthand look, and the *Manchester Guardian* reported on his trip. In 2006 Harris told the *Guardian* that he was impressed by Dutch society's openmindedness. "The attitude I found in the Netherlands was, 'if we give kids all the information and they make mistakes, then it's their responsibility. If we don't give them enough information and they make mistakes, it's our responsibility.'"

Though teen pregnancy rates have continued a steady decline since the turn of the millennium in nearly every part of the world, politicians and policy makers still disagree about the depth of the problem. The authors in this chapter delve into the issue and examine whether it is a serious problem.

Teen Pregnancy Remains a Problem in America

Jonathan D. Klein

Jonathan D. Klein teaches pediatric medicine at the University of Rochester Medical Center in New York.

Each year, approximately 900,000 teenagers become pregnant in the United States, and despite decreasing rates, more than 4 in 10 adolescent girls have been pregnant at least once before 20 years of age. Most of these pregnancies are among older teenagers (ie, those 18 or 19 years of age). Approximately 51% of adolescent pregnancies end in live births, 35% end in induced abortion, and 14% result in miscarriage or stillbirth.

Trends in Adolescent Childbearing

Historically, the highest adolescent birth rates in the United States were during the 1950s and 1960s, before the legalization of abortion and the development of many of the current forms of contraception. After the legalization of abortion in 1973, birth rates for US females 15 to 19 years of age decreased sharply until 1986. Rates increased steadily until 1991; since then, the birth rate among teenagers has decreased every year since 1991. Since 1991, the rate has decreased 35% for 15- to 17-year-olds and 20% for 18- to 19-year-olds. Rates for 10- to 14-year-olds were 1.4 per 1000 in 1992 and have gradually decreased to 0.7 per 1000 in 2002.

Although birth rates have been decreasing steadily for white and black teenagers in recent years, 1996 is the first year that birth rates decreased for Hispanic teenagers; Hispanic adolescents also have had the highest overall birth rates and smallest decreases in recent years.

Jonathan D. Klein, "Adolescent Pregnancy: Current Trends and Issues," *Pediatrics*, vol. 116, no. 1, July 2005, pp. 282–84. Copyright American Academy of Pediatrics. Used with permission.

Once a teenager has had 1 infant, she is at increased risk of having another. Approximately 25% of adolescent births are not first births.

Adolescent Parents and Their Partners

Adolescent childbearing is usually inconsistent with mainstream societal demands for attaining adulthood through education, work experience, and financial stability. Poverty is correlated significantly with adolescent pregnancy in the United States. Although 38% of adolescents live in poor or low-income families, as many as 83% of adolescents who give birth and 61% who have abortions are from poor or low-income families. At least one third of parenting adolescents (both males and females) are themselves products of adolescent pregnancy. Although it is difficult to establish causal links between childhood maltreatment and subsequent adolescent pregnancy, in some studies as many as 50% to 60% of those who become pregnant in early or midadolescence have a history of childhood sexual or physical abuse.

The problem of adolescent pregnancy is often assumed to be both an adolescent and an adult problem, because many partners of childbearing youth are adults. The percentage of adolescent pregnancies in which the father is an adult is unclear; studies report a range from 7% to 67%. Adult men having sexual relationships with adolescents is problematic, because many of these relationships may be abusive or coercive. Adolescents who have sex with older men are also more likely to contract HIV infection or other STDs [sexually transmitted diseases]. Although more than two thirds of adolescent girls' sexual partners are the same age or within a few years older and the sexual activity is consensual in nature, some partners are more than 4 years older. Sexual relationships between adults and minors may be coercive or exploitative, with detrimental consequences for the health of both the teenager and her children. Although some states and local jurisdictions have changed statutory rape laws and their enforcement, mandated reporting of all sexual activity as statutory rape or as child abuse has not been effective at changing behavior, does not allow for clinical judgment, and has the effect of deterring some of the adolescents most in need from seeking health care.

Adolescent fathers are similar to adolescent mothers; they are more likely than their peers who are not fathers to have poor academic performance, higher school drop-out rates, limited financial resources, and decreased income potential. Some fathers disappear from the lives of their adolescent partners and children, but many others attempt to stay involved, and many young fathers struggle to be involved in their children's lives. Current programs in adolescent pregnancy and parenting are exploring ways to reach and engage young fathers in the lives of their children.

More than 90% of 15- to 19-year-olds . . . describe their pregnancies as being unintended.

Single Parenthood Is on the Rise

The birth rate to unmarried female adolescents has been increasing steadily for most of the last 30 years. In 2001, 78.9% of all births to adolescents occurred outside of marriage. The increasing birth rate of unmarried adolescents is primarily attributable to higher rates of births to unmarried white adolescents. However, adolescents account for a smaller percentage of total out-of-wedlock births now (26% in 2001) than they did in 1970 (50%). Births to unmarried teenagers reflect a larger societal trend toward single parenthood, because birth rates for unmarried adults have also increased. Although some reports have suggested that rates of marriage among childbearing teenagers are increasing, few teenagers or young adults who become pregnant are married before their infant is born.

Most Pregnancies Are Unintended

More than 90% of 15- to 19-year-olds (and half of all adults) describe their pregnancies as being unintended. More than half of unintended adolescent pregnancies end in induced or spontaneous abortion, compared with 35% of adolescent pregnancies overall. On the other hand, some adolescent pregnancies are intended, and some young women are motivated to become pregnant and have children. Similar to adults, adolescents give many reasons for wanting to have children; the reason that some adolescents are motivated to be mothers at an early age is unclear. Recent data suggest that many young women are ambivalent about becoming pregnant, and this is associated with less consistent and less effective contraceptive use.

U.S. Teen Birth Rate Remains High

Even with recent decreases, the United States has the highest adolescent birth rate among comparable industrialized countries despite sexual activity rates that are similar or higher among Western European teenagers than among teenagers in the United States. For every 1000 females 15 to 19 years of age in 1992, 4 in Japan gave birth, 8 in the Netherlands gave birth, 33 in the United Kingdom gave birth, 41 in Canada gave birth, and 61 in the United States gave birth. The higher birth rate for American adolescents compared with their peers in other countries is not attributable solely to high birth rates among American minority groups; non-Hispanic white adolescents in the United States also have a higher birth rate than do teenagers observed in any other developed country. The reasons for this contrast are unclear, but European teenagers may have greater access to and acceptance of contraception. The contrast also may be related to universal sexuality education that exists in some European countries. Welfare benefits tend to be more generous in Europe than in the United States;

thus, it is unlikely that the current welfare system motivates or explains American teenagers' decisions to have children.

The incidence of having a low birth weight infant . . . among adolescents is more than double the rate for adults.

Medical Risks of Adolescent Pregnancy

Pregnant adolescents younger than 17 years have a higher incidence of medical complications involving mother and child than do adult women, although these risks may be greatest for the youngest teenagers. The incidence of having a low birth weight infant (<2500 g [5.5 lbs.]) among adolescents is more than double the rate for adults, and the neonatal death rate (within 28 days of birth) is almost 3 times higher. The mortality rate for the mother, although low, is twice that for adult pregnant women.

Adolescent pregnancy has been associated with other medical problems including poor maternal weight gain, prematurity (birth at <37 weeks' gestation), pregnancy-induced hypertension, anemia, and STDs. Approximately 14% of infants born to adolescents 17 years or younger are preterm versus 6% for women 25 to 29 years of age. Young adolescent mothers (14 years and younger) are more likely than other age groups to give birth to underweight infants, and this is more pronounced in black adolescents.

Biological factors that have been associated consistently with negative pregnancy outcomes are poor nutritional status, low prepregnancy weight and height, parity, and poor pregnancy weight gain. Many social factors have also been associated with poor birth outcomes, including poverty, unmarried status, low educational levels, smoking, drug use, and inadequate prenatal care. Both biological and social factors may contribute to poor outcomes in adolescents. Adolescents also have high rates of STDs, substance use, and poor nutritional intake, all of which contribute to the risk of preterm delivery. Interventions, such as prenatal intake of folic acid as a strategy for prevention of spina bifida, can be effective at decreasing observed disparities between adolescents and older women.

Psychosocial Complications of Adolescent Pregnancy

The psychosocial problems of adolescent pregnancy include school interruption, persistent poverty, limited vocational opportunities, separation from the child's father, divorce, and repeat pregnancy. When pregnancy does interrupt an adolescent's education, a history of poor academic performance usually exists. Having repeat births before 18 years of age has a negative effect on high school completion. Factors associated with increased high school completion for pregnant teenagers include race (black teenagers fare better than do white teenagers), being raised in a smaller family, presence of reading materials in the home, employment of the teenager's mother, and having parents with higher educational levels.

Research suggests that long-term negative social outcomes are not inevitable. Several long-term follow-up studies indicate that 2 decades after giving birth, most former adolescent mothers are not welfare-dependent; many have completed high school, have secured regular employment, and do not have large families. Comprehensive adolescent pregnancy programs seem to contribute to good outcomes, as do home-visitation programs designed to promote good child health outcomes.

The Children of Teens Suffer Most

Research during the past decade confirms the common belief that children of adolescent mothers do not fare as well as those of adult mothers. These children have increased risks of developmental delay, academic difficulties, behavioral disorders, substance abuse, early sexual activity, depression, and becoming adolescent parents themselves.

Adolescent mothers may not possess the same level of maternal skills as do adults. There is debate in the literature regarding the association of maternal age and child abuse. Some studies indicate that young maternal age is a risk factor for abuse, including fatalities, and others indicate the presence of reporting biases that may confound the findings.

Although the current political climate tends to require that adolescent mothers live at home with their own families to qualify for government assistance, there is evidence that intensive involvement of families in rearing children of older adolescents may not be beneficial for either the adolescent or her child. Many adolescent parenting programs are exploring ways to involve the families of the parenting adolescent in child care activities that are helpful.

Adolescent Pregnancy Prevention Should Be a Priority

Many models of adolescent pregnancy-prevention programs exist. Most successful programs include multiple and varied approaches to the problem and include abstinence promotion and contraception information, contraceptive availability, sexuality education, school-completion strategies, and job training. Primary-prevention (first pregnancy) and secondary-prevention (repeat pregnancy) programs are both needed, with particular attention to adolescents who are at highest risk of becoming pregnant and innovative programs that include males. Parents, schools, religious institutions, physicians, social and government agencies, and adolescents all have roles in successful prevention programs.

Efforts to prevent adolescent pregnancy at both the national and local levels have increased in recent years, and there has been increasing evidence that several different kinds of programs may help decrease sexual risk taking and pregnancy among teenagers. Recent studies have found that some sexuality- and HIV-education programs have sustained positive effects on behavior, and at least 1 program that combines sexuality education and youth development has been shown to decrease pregnancy rates for as long as 3 years. Additionally, both community learning programs and sexuality- and HIV-education programs have been found to decrease sexual risk taking and/or pregnancy, and short clinic-based interventions involving educational materials coupled with counseling also may increase contraceptive use.

Despite encouraging trends, efforts to prevent pregnancy must be constantly renewed as children enter into adolescence. By 2010, the population of adolescent girls 15 to 19 years of age is expected to increase by 10%; thus, decreasing pregnancy rates may not mean fewer pregnancies or births. Nonetheless, condom use has increased slightly, and adolescent contraceptive users have increasingly adopted long-acting hormonal methods, which have the lowest failure rates; thus, overall contraceptive effectiveness among teenagers has been improving.

Current research indicates that encouraging abstinence and urging better use of contraception are compatible goals. Evidence shows that sexuality education that discusses contraception does not increase sexual activity, and programs that emphasize abstinence as the safest and best approach, while also teaching about contraceptives for sexually active youth, do not decrease contraceptive use.

Teen Pregnancy Has Negative Consequences for Mother, Child, and Society

National Campaign to Prevent Teen Pregnancy

Founded in 1996, the National Campaign to Prevent Teen Pregnancy is a nonprofit, nonpartisan organization that seeks to improve the lives of children, youth, and their families by reducing teen pregnancy. The organization does this by bringing awareness to the issue on the national level as well as providing assistance and resources to those already working on the issue.

The National Campaign to Prevent Teen Pregnancy, organized in 1996, is based on the concept that reducing the nation's rate of teen pregnancy is one of the most strategic and direct means available to improve overall child well-being and to reduce persistent child poverty. Teen pregnancy has serious consequences for the teen mother, the child, and to society in general.

Despite the recently declining teen pregnancy rates, 35% of teenage girls get pregnant at least once before they reach age 20, resulting in 850,000 teen pregnancies each year. At this level, the United States has the highest rate of teen pregnancy in the fully industrialized world.

Teen Pregnancy Is Bad for the Mother

- *Future prospects for teenagers decline significantly if they have a baby.* Teen mothers are less likely to complete school and more likely to be single parents. Less than one-third of teens who begin their families before age 18 ever earn a high school diploma and only 1.5% earn a college degree by the age of 30.

National Campaign to Prevent Teen Pregnancy, "Teen Pregnancy—So What?" teenpregnancy.org, February 2004. Reproduced by permission.

- *There are serious health risks for adolescents who have babies.* Common medical problems among adolescent mothers include poor weight gain, pregnancy-induced hypertension, anemia, sexually transmitted diseases (STDs), and cephalopelvic disproportion [a condition in which a baby is too big to fit through its mother's pelvis for a natural birth]. Later in life, adolescent mothers tend to be at greater risk for obesity and hypertension than women who were not teenagers when they had their first child.

- *Teen pregnancy is closely linked to poverty and single parenthood.* A 1990 study showed that almost one-half of all teenage mothers and over three-quarters of *unmarried* teen mothers began receiving welfare within five years of the birth of their first child. The growth in single-parent families remains the single most important reason for increased poverty among children over the last twenty years, as documented in the 1998 Economic Report of the President. Out-of-wedlock childbearing (as opposed to divorce) is currently the driving force behind the growth in the number of single parents, and half of first out-of-wedlock births are to teens. Therefore, reducing teen pregnancy and childbearing is an obvious place to anchor serious efforts to reduce poverty in future generations.

Children of teens are 50 percent more likely to repeat a grade.

Teen Pregnancy Is Bad for the Child

- *Children born to teen mothers suffer from higher rates of low birth weight and related health problems.* The proportion of babies with low birth weights born to teens is 21 percent higher than the proportion for mothers age 20–24. Low birth weight raises the probabilities of infant death, blindness, deafness, chronic respiratory problems, mental retardation, mental illness, and cerebral palsy. In addition, low birth weight doubles the chances that a child will later be diagnosed as having dyslexia, hyperactivity, or another disability.

- *Children of teens often have insufficient health care.* Despite having more health problems than the children of older mothers, the children of teen mothers receive less medical care and treatment. In his or her first 14 years, the average child of a teen mother visits a physician and other medical providers an average of 3.8 times per year, compared with 4.3 times for a child of older childbearers. And when they do visit medical providers, more of the expenses they incur are paid by others in society. One recent study suggested that the medical expenses paid by society would be reduced dramatically if teenage mothers were to wait until they were older to have their first child.

- *Children of teen mothers often receive inadequate parenting.* Children born to teen mothers are at higher risk of poor parenting because their mothers—and often their fathers as well—are typically too young to master the demanding job of being a parent. Still growing and developing themselves, teen mothers are often unable to provide the kind of environment that infants and very young children require for optimal development. Recent research, for example, has clarified the critical importance of sensitive parenting and early cognitive stimulation for adequate brain development. Given the importance of careful nurturing and stimulation in the first three years of life, the burden born by babies with parents who are too young to be in this role is especially great.

- *Children with adolescent parents often fall victim to abuse and neglect.* A recent analysis found that there are 110 reported incidents of abuse and neglect per 1,000 families headed by a young teen mother. By contrast, in families where the mothers delay childbearing until their early twenties, the rate is less than half this level—or 51 incidents per 1,000 families. Similarly, rates of foster care placement are significantly higher for children whose mothers are under 18. In fact, over half of foster care placements of children with these young mothers could be averted by delaying childbearing, thereby saving taxpayers nearly $1 billion annually in foster care costs alone.

- *Children of teenagers often suffer from poor school performance.* Children of teens are 50 percent more likely to repeat a grade; they perform much worse on standardized tests; and ultimately they are less likely to complete high school than if their mothers had delayed childbearing.

Each year the federal government alone spends about $40 billion to help families that began with a teenage birth.

And Bad for Us All

- *The U.S. still leads the fully industrialized world in teen pregnancy and birth rates—by a wide margin.* In fact, the U.S. rates are nearly double Great Britain's, at least four times those of France and Germany, and more than ten times that of Japan.

- *Teen pregnancy costs society billions of dollars a year.* There are nearly half a million children born to teen mothers each year. Most of these mothers are unmarried, and many will end up poor and on welfare. Each year the federal government alone spends about $40 billion to help families that began with a teenage birth.

- *Teen pregnancy hurts the business community's "bottom line."* Too many children start school unprepared to learn, and teachers are overwhelmed trying to deal with problems that start in the home. Forty-five percent of first births in the United States are to women who are either unmarried, teenagers, or lacking a high school degree, which means that too many children— tomorrow's workers—are born into families that are not prepared to help them succeed. In addition, teen mothers often do not finish high school themselves. It's not easy for a teen to learn work skills and be a dependable employee while caring for children.

- *A new crop of kids becomes teenagers each year.* This means that prevention efforts must be constantly renewed and reinvented. And between 1995 and 2010, the number of girls aged 15–19 is projected to increase by 2.2 million.

Teen Pregnancy Causes Family Stress

Susan S. Bartell

Susan S. Bartell is a licensed psychologist who specializes in the issues of parents and children. She is the author of Mommy or Daddy: Whose Side Am I On?

Each year approximately one million teenage girls become pregnant—10% of all girls ages 15–19, and 19% of those who are sexually active. Furthermore, 13% of all births in the United States are to teenage girls. Given these numbers, teen pregnancy is clearly a far-reaching issue, and one that could affect those working in the areas of pregnancy and childbirth.

But, despite these statistics, most people in the western world experience the pregnancy of a teenage girl as a surprising, and usually upsetting or even scandalous, occurrence. It impacts tremendously on an entire family system, beginning with the pregnant teen and extending to everyone in the family who becomes a part of the process of the pregnancy and its outcome.

Teen Pregnancy Is Usually an Accident

For many teens, becoming pregnant appears to be an accident. Statistics indicate that about three-fourths of teen pregnancies are unintended. Some girls have incorrect information as to how to prevent pregnancy (e.g., if a boy "pulls out" before ejaculating; if she douches after sex; if she has her period), leading to accidental pregnancy. Others behave irresponsibly, or impulsively, choose to have intercourse "just this once" without a condom, or forget to take birth control pills frequently enough.

Susan S. Bartell, "Teen Pregnancy: The Impact on a Family System," *International Journal of Childbirth Education*, vol. 20, no. 2, June 2005, pp. 19–21. Reproduced by permission.

However, for many girls, a subconscious desire to become pregnant actually drives them to behave in ways that will, in fact, result in them becoming pregnant. This group is likely to account for a good percentage of the "accidental pregnancy" statistics, which appear to be the result of naïve or impulsive decisions to have unprotected intercourse. Clinically, this is seen by those who work with teens. Many girls typically have unprotected intercourse frequently, not just once in a while, thereby dramatically increasing their chances of becoming pregnant. They may report that a pregnancy was accidental, but for many the drive to become pregnant is real, although perhaps not even recognized by the girl herself. In addition, many girls (including those who seem naïve at first) are fully aware of the way in which pregnancy occurs, but choose to ignore these facts.

If one examines the developmental tasks of adolescence, a subconscious desire to become pregnant is actually consistent with the stereotypical teenage struggle between becoming independent and remaining attached to her parents. In many ways the pregnancy and potential baby represent a transitional object for the girl as she moves towards adulthood. For this girl, the baby is "guaranteed" to remain attached to her, even as she is growing up and feeling that she is losing her parents. A teen is particularly susceptible to becoming pregnant when her bond with a parent is tenuous already, or if her parent is physically or emotionally unavailable to her. The need for a secure bond with another person becomes overwhelming and when a parent is unable to provide this security, she attempts to create (literally) a new bond for herself.

Some Girls Desire Pregnancy

For a teen who is struggling emotionally with the transition to adulthood, without the support of a parent, a baby represents a re-creation of her own childhood, a chance to parent her child in the way she wishes she had been parented herself. For a girl who has had a damaged childhood, this can become a very compelling reason for her to become pregnant. The need to redo childhood; to give to her child what she feels was never given to her emotionally—love, affection, attention—can be overwhelming.

Another reason that a teen may subconsciously, or even with full awareness, become pregnant is that she believes (erroneously, of course) that pregnancy will ensure her continued relationship with the father of the child she is carrying. This intense desire for guaranteed closeness arises from the feeling that separation is a scary, rather than an exciting process. When a girl feels this, it is likely that she did not have a secure primary attachment to her parents prior to adolescence. Now, as a teenager, when she feels compelled to separate from them, she has a strong desire to bond securely with another person who can meet her needs. In this case, it is the baby's father with whom she feels an intimate connection based on their sexual and sometimes emotional relationship. She is desperate for a secure attachment and hopes that the child will ensure this bond between herself and him.

Many experience early pregnancy as a terrifying endeavor, with . . . a sense of responsibility almost too great to bear.

Early Pregnancy May Cause Emotional Turmoil

Regardless of whether a girl becomes pregnant truly by accident, whether it is subconsciously deliberate or whether it is a conscious choice, it is unlikely that she will be prepared for the emotional shifts within herself as the pregnancy develops. As with grown women, the physical changes, as well as the overwhelming notion that she is carrying a living, growing human being, can be fantastic and also confusing; however, unlike grown women, girls do not have the emotional maturity to grapple with these issues in a way that is always positive.

For some, the sense of responsibility is too much. A girl may deny the existence of the pregnancy for as long as possible (in rare cases, this can be until giving birth). In the first several months she may also be terrified to tell a parent or another adult of the pregnancy, thereby denying herself the opportunity to speak about fears, worries, physical changes, or plans. Most teens do not read pregnancy books or understand the changes that are taking place within themselves. For these reasons, many experience early pregnancy as a terrifying endeavor, with little support, a seemingly endless fear of the unknown, and a sense of responsibility almost too great to bear.

The emotional stress of having to decide to carry or terminate a pregnancy can be a tremendous burden for a teenager.

Opting for an Abortion

At some point in early pregnancy most teens grapple with the question of whether or not to terminate the pregnancy. For many, particularly those for whom the pregnancy is fulfilling a deep, subconscious wish, termination seems out of the question. This is true for those with strong religious convictions as well. But despite this, the fear of childbirth, the fear of her parents finding out, or the awesome responsibility of bringing a child into the world, causes almost every girl to give some thought to ending the pregnancy, despite the psychological or religious reasons for wanting to keep the pregnancy.

Currently, about 40% of teens choose to end a pregnancy with abortion. This rate has been slowly declining due to lower pregnancy rates, as well as to fewer teens choosing abortion. For some teens abortion is not an option because they reveal or admit to their pregnancy too late to be able to terminate safely. For these, carrying to term is the only choice.

The emotional stress of having to decide to carry or terminate a pregnancy can be a tremendous burden for a teenager. This is made even more severe if a parent, social pressure, or religious or moral concerns are attempting to sway her in one direction or another. Until the decision is made, it can consume a girl's thoughts completely, whether or not she has told anyone of the pregnancy. It is also a decision that can emotionally impact a girl far into adulthood. As an adult, looking back on a teen pregnancy, a woman may wish that she had made a different decision, depending upon the outcome she is now experiencing. Of course as a teen, she could not have known that she would pine for the lost child or, alternatively, feel that the child had been an enormous burden.

A great many women who relinquished a newborn as a teen continue as an adult to experience feelings of loss.

Choosing Adoption

The decision to maintain the pregnancy but then give the baby up for adoption will also result in a traumatic experience for the teen. If she desired the pregnancy, either consciously or subconsciously, having to give up the baby will be experienced as a tremendous and devastating loss. But unlike abortion, adoption is not typically a decision a teen makes alone. If she carries her pregnancy to term, it is unlikely that she will be able to hide it, or the baby (although, not impossible in some situations). At some point her parents will help her to decide, or even insist upon her either keeping the baby or giving it up for adoption. Interestingly, less than 10% of teens ultimately place their babies for adoption (National Committee for Adoption 1989). There are many reasons for this, one of which is the tremendous loss that the girl would feel having to give up her baby, particularly if the baby is playing a significant emotional role in the girl's adolescence.

For those girls who choose, or are forced by their parents, to give up a baby for adoption, a great deal of emotional support is needed, for quite some time after the birth and adoption. Professional counseling is strongly recommended for an extended period to help her cope with the loss, as well as the subconscious issues that often come to the surface with the birth. If a teen loses a pregnancy, counseling may also be necessary to cope with the loss, although the issues will not be as profound as those of a teen who carried a baby to term and then chose to give it up.

A great many women who relinquished a newborn as a teen continue as an adult to experience feelings of loss, often fantasizing about a relationship with the child they gave away, experiencing guilt, and sometimes expressing regret about their decision as well. A woman may also feel resentment towards her own parent(s) if she feels that she was coerced into making the decision to give up the baby for adoption. It is nonetheless possible for these feelings to coexist with the knowledge that, in fact, giving up the child was actually the right decision.

Transitioning to Motherhood

For those families of teens who choose to keep the baby, typically a great deal of adjustment is required by the teen as she must shed her old identity as carefree teenager and enter the new role of motherhood. When a girl's parents take on the lion's share of caring for the new baby, this shift is not as dramatic as it is for a girl who must do most, or all, of the parenting work herself. But in either case, becoming a mother challenges the very same drive for independence that resulted in the pregnancy in the first place. It emphasizes attachment, places the focus on childhood (albeit not her own), and stifles the girl's ability to move forward with her life. Indeed, according to studies, nearly 80% of teen mothers eventually go on welfare, a testimony to the stranglehold that teen parenthood can have upon a girl, making it difficult for her to move ahead in her life.

Adolescent Pregnancy Causes Family Conflict

In many discussions of teen pregnancy, the impact on the girl's family goes unrecognized. In fact, having a pregnant daughter can evoke a considerable number of feelings for a pregnant girl's parents. To begin with, pregnancy brings a parent face-to-face with a daughter's sexuality, which, up until this time, has likely been easy to avoid confronting directly. Although a parent may not truly have considered the daughter to be sexually inexperienced, a tacit agreement often exists between parent and teen (rightly or wrongly) that "as long as it isn't obvious, we can pretend it's not happening." A pregnancy violates this agreement, forcing a parent to have uncomfortable knowledge. Many a parent reacts to this knowledge with anger directed at his or her daughter.

For most parents, there develops an enormous emotional struggle between feeling angry and betrayed by a daughter and wanting to take care of her.

The anger, at least initially, is at the betrayal of the pretense, or reality, of innocence, rather than with the actual pregnancy. For these parents, the loss of a daughter's childhood is sometimes felt as a sign that they are aging, a far greater issue than many parents are able to admit. Some parents also confront the idea that they have somehow failed their daughter, causing her pregnancy. Being forced to face this conflict may make them feel uncomfortable, guilty, or even angry with the girl for somehow evoking the feeling by becoming pregnant.

For a minority of parents, the pregnancy will be welcomed as a positive addition to the family or as a rite of passage for the teenager, into adulthood. In most cases though, once the initial shock wears off, the pregnancy will be viewed as deeply troubling, and reflective of a teenager gone badly awry. The emotional struggles as to whether to terminate the pregnancy or not, and then later, as to whether to keep the baby or not, will continue in the family until resolution is reached, which could take weeks or months, resulting in enormous emotional upheaval, particularly if the teen and her parent do not see eye-to-eye on the resolution.

Parents Grapple with Love and Anger

For most parents, there develops an enormous emotional struggle between feeling angry and betrayed by a daughter and wanting to take care of her and nurture her through her pregnancy. For some parents, the desire to nurture prevails, which, while positive in one regard, conversely suggests to her that becoming pregnant was not a mistake since it garnered her the attention and care of her parent (sometimes for the first time in years).

The path of a pregnant teen is rarely one that is stress-free and joyful.

Ironically, when the baby is born the new grandparent may shower the baby with affection, while the teen is once again relegated to feeling less than consequential in the life of her mother or father. Indeed, in many families, the teen's mother becomes the primary caretaker for the baby, intending to free up her daughter to continue in her own adolescent life with as little interruption as possible. The teen's parent(s) may not realize that given the teen's need for emotional attachment, this is not what she had in mind—hoping instead to nurture her own relationship with the baby.

Teen Pregnancy Is a Time of Stress

There can be conflicts between the teen and her mother that interfere with the teen's ability to nurture her own relationship with her child. Sometimes this happens because the teen's mother doesn't want her daughter tied down by a baby, and sometimes it happens because the teen's mother wants the opportunity to raise another child—perhaps she feels that she will do a better job this time. Or, perhaps she feels jealous that her daughter is at the beginning of her childbearing years, while, as the mother of a teenager, she may be closer to the end of her own.

The path of a pregnant teen is rarely one that is stress-free and joyful. For most, there is little real support—financial or emotional—from an immature and often resentful partner. Her parents are shocked and she is confused at the enormity of the position in which she finds herself. For a pregnant teen, the professionals with whom she works throughout this difficult time in her life have the opportunity to be a source of comfort, support, and information, offered without judgment.

Teen Pregnancy Is Not a Public Health Problem

Debbie A. Lawlor and Mary Shaw

Debbie A. Lawlor teaches epidemiology and public health in the Department of Social Medicine at Britain's University of Bristol. Mary Shaw is the science director of the department's South West Public Health Observatory.

Debates about the appropriate age at which a woman should become a mother are not new, but it is only in recent decades that, in Britain at least, teenage pregnancy has become labelled alongside cardiovascular disease, cancer and mental health as a major public health problem. . . . We . . . argue that teenage pregnancy should not be conceptualized as a public health problem and suggest that this label is rather a reflection of what is considered to be—in this time and place—socially, culturally and economically acceptable.

The management of reproduction and childbirth has, in most countries and most cultures, been the province of women, but the rise of western biomedicine in the 18th century and its consolidation in the 19th led to the medicalization of pregnancy. This process was important not only in terms of shifting gender roles in medical care, but because it signalled a shift of power relations by which women's bodies and the reproductive process came to be seen as legitimate subjects for social control. This is exemplified in the development of public health policies during the 1990s, in Britain and the US, which have included teenage pregnancy as a national public health problem requiring targeted interventions. The concern of both countries relates to their rates of teenage pregnancy being higher than those in other developed coun-

Debbie A. Lawlor and Mary Shaw, "Too Much Too Young? Teenage Pregnancy Is Not a Public Health Problem," *International Journal of Epidemiology*, 2002, pp. 552–53. Copyright © 2002 Oxford University Press. Reproduced by permission of the publisher and author.

tries. However, the idea that teenage pregnancy constitutes a health problem is expressed in policy documents in many developed countries, regardless of whether they have a relatively high rate. For example, the Nordic Resolution on Adolescent Sexual Health Rights counts as a measure of public health success the fact that 'the number of teenage pregnancies in Nordic [Scandinavian] countries are among the lowest in the world'.

Most teenage pregnancies are low risk—a point which is omitted from much research and from policy documents and statements.

Does Age Really Matter?

A crucial question relates to whether the adverse outcomes experienced by (some) mothers and children of teenage pregnancies are causally related to the *age* of the mother, or whether there are other factors which lead to the adverse outcomes experienced by teenage mothers and their children. Several studies have found that teenage pregnancy is associated with adverse outcomes for both mother and baby. These include low birthweight, prematurity, increased perinatal and infant mortality and poorer long-term cognitive development and educational achievement for both mother and child. However, studies which have aimed to address the underlying causes of these adverse outcomes—by controlling for additional factors—have produced conflicting results. Some suggest that adverse outcomes remain even after controlling for maternal socioeconomic position and other confounding factors, some find that age has no effect, whereas other studies report that once maternal socioeconomic position and smoking are taken into account young age is actually associated with *better* outcomes.

These contradictory findings probably reflect the small size of some studies, residual confounding, and the difficulty of separating effects that may be related to maternal age from effects that are appropriately regarded as confounding. For example, poor parenting skills may reflect the ignorance of young age but may also occur at any age among women who have restricted access to information and education. Larger studies and those employing methods specifically designed to adequately control for confounding factors (for example using sibling comparisons) suggest that young age is *not* an important determinant of pregnancy outcome or of the future health of the mother. A recent systematic review of the medical consequences of teenage pregnancy concluded that 'critical appraisal suggested that increased risks of these outcomes [anaemia, pregnancy-induced hypertension, low birthweight, prematurity, intra-uterine growth retardation and neonatal mortality] were predominantly caused by the social, economic, and behavioural factors that predispose some young women to pregnancy.' Moreover, [A.J.] Cunnington [of the University of Oxford Medical School] asserts from this review that most teenage pregnancies are low risk—a point which is omitted from much research and from policy documents and statements.

Attitudes towards young mothers . . . shift in relation to prevailing moral values.

Studies Are Inconclusive

In addition, and this is perhaps more the case than with other public health issues, it is problematic to transpose the findings of studies across different populations (or indeed different times). For example, black American teenage mothers are no less likely to breastfeed than are older mothers, whereas fewer white teenage mothers breastfeed; in one study low birthweight was found to be associated with teenage pregnancy amongst white but not black mothers. Good pregnancy outcomes have been found amongst teenage mothers (age 15–19 years) from an ultraorthodox Jewish community living in Jerusalem [Israel] amongst whom marriage and pregnancy at a young age is encouraged and the women strongly supported within the community. Attitudes towards young mothers (and towards lone [single] mothers, these groups often overlapping) shift in relation to prevailing moral values, and also to some extent reflect economic conditions. The experiences of teenage mothers may, to an extent, be a sign of the prevailing values of health care professionals and society more generally. Hence poor outcomes in one population, even with adequate control for confounding factors, may reflect the attitudes of that particular society towards teenage pregnancy and motherhood. It has been suggested that the findings of poor perinatal outcomes amongst teenage mothers in one study conducted in Utah, despite control for a range of socioeconomic factors, may be explained by the very low prevalence of teenage pregnancy in Utah: 'Thus being a teenage mother in Utah is unusual, even under optimal circumstances.'

It has been suggested that a large proportion of teenage pregnancies are unintended and that many may be the result of abuse. But surely unintended pregnancy or pregnancy that is the result of abuse is something that should concern health professionals regardless of the age of the mother? In the US it is estimated that one-third of all pregnancies that result in live births are unintended. This is clearly not something that affects only teenage mothers, and whether 'unintended' pregnancy is detrimental to either baby or mother has not been established.

Risks of Older Motherhood Overlooked

It is important to consider whether labelling *teenage* pregnancy as a public health problem affords any benefit to mothers or children. What public health impact would we achieve [asks S.D. Hoffman in an article in volume 30 of *Family Planning Perspectives*,] '... if we could successfully intervene and change a woman's age at first birth and *nothing else* about her up to that point'?

There is no convincing evidence that teenage pregnancy is a public health problem.

In the developed world it is increasingly common for women to delay their first birth until they are in their thirties—indeed the mean age of first birth for married women in England and Wales was 29.3 in 1999. Across Western Europe the age of first-time mothers is at an all time high, which demographers attribute to social and economic factors such as female and male wages and career planning on the part of women. This trend is despite the increased risk of chromosomal abnormalities and complications of pregnancy in the 30+ age group. Furthermore, it is not often recognized that maternal mortality increases exponentially with mother's age. Women having babies in their thirties and forties are not labelled a 'public health problem', and neither are women who receive (or more usually, can pay for) infertility treatment, even though their babies have an increased risk of perinatal death. The 'risks' that are seen as pertinent vary with the age of the mother—any health risks to older women may be disregarded by public policy makers as older mothers are more likely to be educated, economically self-reliant and from a higher socioeconomic class. Interestingly, it has been argued that for older women the poorer medical outcomes associated with older maternal age may be disregarded because of the better social outcomes for children of older women.

Teen Pregnancy Concerns Are Overrated

There is no convincing evidence that teenage pregnancy is a public health problem and it is difficult to identify a biologically plausible reason for adverse outcomes of young maternal age, as Cunnington says: 'It makes little biological sense for young women to be able to reproduce at an age that puts their children at risk.' For policy makers the labelling of teenage pregnancy as a public health problem reflects social, cultural and economic imperatives. Researchers and health practitioners should think more carefully about why something is labelled a public health problem, together with the social and moral context in which it occurs and in which they practice.

British Prime Minister Tony Blair's preface to the Social Exclusion Unit's report on teenage pregnancy indicates the strength of negative feelings:

> While the rate of teenage pregnancies has remained high here, throughout most of the rest of Western Europe it fell rapidly. As a country, we can't afford to continue to ignore this shameful record.

We do not agree that teenage pregnancy is shameful, nor do we believe that teenage pregnancy is (or is best conceptualized as) a public health problem; however, we do believe that the accumulative effect of social and economic exclusion on the health of mothers and their babies, whatever their age, is.

Early Parenthood Improves Some Teens' Lives

Kim Phillips-Fein

Kim Phillips-Fein is a professor at New York University's Gallatin School of Individualized Study and has authored many articles for various publications.

Everybody loves a teenage mother. Whether firebrand conservative or bleeding-heart liberal, if you've got a typewriter and a pose to strike quickly, she's your gal. . . . A *Newsweek* cover story summed up what everybody knows about teen motherhood: "The Name of the Game Is Shame."

Studying Cause and Effect

A study done by University of Chicago professor Joseph Hotz may force the moralizers to do some rethinking. In the public debate on teen motherhood, the causal relationship between early childbearing and low income is taken to be axiomatic. Teen mothers stay poor because they're "kids having kids"; with the proper self-esteem classes and a couple of condoms, or lectures on abstinence from a stern patriarch, they'd be sure to be living better lives. It's true that teen mothers are, on average, poorer and have lower levels of educational achievement than the general population. But correlation is not causation, as the statisticians say. Do women become poor because they have children as teenagers? Or do they have children as teenagers because they're poor?

In order to test whether convincing teenage mothers to delay birth will actually improve their educational achievements and income levels, Hotz designed a model that would isolate the variable of pregnancy, showing what would happen to a woman in all other respects similar to a teen mother—except that she had not given birth as a teenager. He analyzed data from the National Longitudinal Study of Youth (a project started in 1979 that interviews groups of teenagers on an annual basis throughout their lifetimes), using as the control group teenagers who become pregnant but miscarry, and then wait to have their first child between ages 20 and 25. These are women who behave the way they would if we had a perfectly designed, perfectly targeted program to stop teen pregnancy, a program that brought the teen birthrate down to zero. But compared to this control group, teenage mothers actually achieve higher levels of economic success: They earn more money and work more hours than they would have had they waited to have children.

Hotz's study found teen mothers to be, predictably, less likely to work long hours during their teenage years, when their children are young. But once they hit their 20s, teenage mothers work roughly 1,000 hours a year—approximately 100 to 200 hours a year more than they would have if they had delayed childbearing. . . . Teenage motherhood has a similar effect on earnings. Early childbearing initially depresses the labor market earnings of teenage mothers by about $2,500 a year. However, by the time these women reach their 20s, they are earning approximately $5,000 more than they would have if they had delayed their childbearing. According to Hotz, teenage mothers earn an average of $11,000 a year at 25 and $19,000 at 30—insufficient salaries for raising a family decently, but not exactly scraping change from the gutter, either. The kinds of jobs low-income women frequently hold—as secretaries, nurse's aides, telephone receptionists—value seniority and experience over credentials. Interrupting a service-sector job to take care of young children is more harmful to mothers' salaries than taking time off from high school is.

No Bed of Roses

Hotz's study leaves plenty of room for naysayers who want to remind us of the obvious—that teenage motherhood is no bed of roses. While they're likely to obtain a GED [high school diploma equivalent] in their late teens or 20s, teenage mothers are less likely to ever finish high school than those who wait to have kids. Women who bear children extremely young, under age 15, suffer much more severe setbacks in the labor market.

In a perfect world, reproductive freedom wouldn't mean only the power to protect oneself from unplanned pregnancy, but access to the resources that make it possible for a woman to raise a child at whatever point in her life cycle she deems best. But in the world we live in, not even the first condition fully applies. Teen pregnancy can't be ascribed merely to accidents or bad planning, let alone some cultural pathology haunting us from the days of slavery; given the employment prospects for many poor women, it can be a rational response to a difficult situation. As for the problems of the inner city, there isn't any secret formula that accounts for them all—if we want to do something about falling wages and failing schools, we need to talk about the economy and the educational system, and leave the teen mothers alone.

Early Parenthood Can Push Struggling Teens to Succeed

Jennifer A. Hurley

Jennifer A. Hurley writes and edits reference books for young adults and teens.

Virtually every discussion of teen pregnancy relies on the same implicit assumption: Pregnancy ruins teens' lives. From the way the issue is portrayed by the media, one would think that pregnancy consigned teens to lives of misery, destitution, and regret.

The experience of Angle Hernandez, a teen mother residing in Tampa Bay, Florida, however, belies this view. At seventeen, she lives happily with her baby Anthony and her husband Joshua, the baby's father. She is working toward her equivalency diploma and plans to attend college. "I don't miss anything from my old life," she says. "I'm glad this happened."

A surprisingly large number of teen parents say the same thing. One teenage girl declares that the times spent with her infant have been "the best of her life." A young man who was involved in drugs and crime before his girlfriend became pregnant states, "I like being a father and having a family. It's a challenge."

Meeting the Challenge of Parenthood

Most adults assume that parenthood "ruins" teens' lives by burdening them with responsibility at too young an age. In reality, many teens find that the challenge of parenthood vastly *improves* their lives. Instead of limiting their opportunities, parenthood actually motivates many teens to work harder and to expect more from their lives than they would have otherwise. As Terry Parks, an eighteen-year-old with a two-year-old son, explains, "My child . . . gives me a reason to keep going and to strive for more. . . . The thought that he's there, too, is what really gives me that push to do more for myself. He's a good boy. He's saved my life in a lot of ways."

Dana Little, who became pregnant at age fifteen, makes a similar comment about her son: "He gives me a push, makes me strive to do better. . . . He's been very positive in my life."

In many cases, the desire to be a good parent acts as a powerful incentive for young people to abandon a destructive lifestyle—one that involves drinking, drug abuse, or promiscuous sex, for example—in favor of a responsible one. Many teens who had performed poorly in school before their pregnancies become focused on educational and career goals after having a baby. Scholar Kristin Luker writes that

> Some young women say [that having a child] was the best thing they ever did. In a few cases it leads to marriage or a stable relationship; in many others it motivates a woman to push herself for her baby's sake; and in still other cases it enhances the woman's self-esteem, since it enables her to do something productive, something nurturing and socially responsible.

For Some, a Way Out

Moreover, for the thousands of teens who suffer abuse each year, pregnancy is one of the few means of escape from their abusers. In fact, a large proportion of teenage girls who become pregnant live in troubled homes or experience sexual, physical, or emotional abuse at the hands of family members. Sociologist Mike Males reports that

> [A] study of pregnant teens and teenaged mothers showed that two-thirds had been raped or sexually abused, nearly always by parents, other guardians, or relatives. Six in ten teen mothers' childhoods also included severe physical vio-

By making the commitment to follow through with academics, teen mothers can make a better life for themselves and their babies. These teen mothers graduated from The New Futures School in Albuquerque, New Mexico, in 1995. Getty Images.

lence: being beaten with a stick, strap, or fist, thrown against walls, deprived of food, locked in closets, or burned with cigarettes or hot water.

Many abused teens find that pregnancy gives them an opportunity to improve their situation. Pregnancy often motivates these teens to leave home so as not to subject their new babies to an abusive home life. Some end up at emergency shelters for pregnant mothers, where they stay until they complete school and find a stable living situation. Yale Gancherov, a supervising social worker at the Crittenton Center for Young Women in Los Angeles, contends that the teen mothers who reside at the center are better off than they were before they became pregnant: "The parents of these young women were violent, were drug abusers, were sexually abusive, were absent or neglectful. While privileged people may see a detriment in a teenager becoming a mother, these girls see it as a realistic improvement in their lives."

Almonica, a sixteen-year-old pregnant teen, came to the Crittenton Center having recently witnessed her stepfather burn her mother to death during a drunken fight. Almonica says that getting pregnant was her "way out" of what could be a similar fate.

Not a Tragedy

Cases like Almonica's, in which teen pregnancy was a positive step, are rarely mentioned because they do not send the "appropriate" message to teens about teen pregnancy. However, it is wrong to misrepresent the effects of teen pregnancy, even for the purpose of discouraging teens from parenthood. Although pregnancy is certainly not the best choice for most teens, it is also not the tragedy that it is made out to be. Society should stop demonizing teen parents and instead recognize them as human beings struggling to meet the challenges life brings them—and often doing so successfully and happily.

CHAPTER 2

What Factors Contribute to Teen Pregnancy?

Chapter Preface

Teen pregnancy remains one of the touchiest social and political issues of the time. Politicians, columnists, educators, and researchers spar over the causes—and extent—of the problem, and each week headlines proclaim that new research has uncovered new factors contributing to the phenomenon.

In recent years some researchers have focused their attention on the media, wondering if a diet of television high in sexual content contributes to teen sex and pregnancy. In the September 2004 issue of the medical journal *Pediatrics*, a group of researchers report on their longitudinal study into the matter. The researchers conclude that "watching sex on TV predicts and may hasten adolescent sexual initiation."

For the study, researchers interviewed nearly two thousand adolescents one year and conducted a follow-up interview the next. They conclude that, compared with children who watch little television sex, children who have a lot of exposure to sexual content on television are about twice as likely to begin having intercourse within the following year.

According to the *Philadelphia Inquirer*, sex is depicted in about two-thirds of all shows, excluding sports and news, and the average teen watches three hours of these shows per day. The *Pediatrics* report notes that the sexual content therefore "may create the illusion that sex is more central to daily life than it truly is and may promote sexual initiation as a result."

In July 2005 *Pediatrics* followed up with another report, this time looking at all media, including music, movies, the Internet, and video games. That report noted that 83 percent of the television programs most frequently watched by teens include sexual content, with an average of 6.7 scenes per hour that include sexual topics. As to the effect this has on teenagers, the report concluded that adolescents exposed to television sex are more likely to have permissive attitudes toward premarital sex. The researchers also noted that more studies are needed to look at the long-term cumulative effects of mass media exposure to sex to see how it affects teens' attitudes and behaviors.

While many politicians and policy makers seem to have clear ideas about what influences contribute to teen pregnancy, the reality may be somewhat murkier. The factors that contribute to teen pregnancy are complicated and overlapping, as some of the authors in this chapter reveal.

Poverty and Lack of Academic Success Contribute to Teen Pregnancy

Carol Cassell

Carol Cassell is the former president of the American Association of Sex Educators and director of a private consulting practice, Critical Pathways, which provides technical support on teen pregnancy prevention. Critical Pathways is located in Albuquerque, New Mexico.

Although it is difficult to untangle the pathway of adolescent parenthood from the intricate web of economic, cultural, and social forces that influence the life course of an adolescent, it is abundantly clear that the factors influencing a teenager at risk for pregnancy intersect at the crossroads of poverty and academic achievement. Of course, not all pregnancies or school academic problems lead to adolescent parenthood or to dropping out of school. Still, there is mounting evidence that these problems share common roots and consequences, and often a student with one of these problems will be a candidate for the other.

School dropout problems and school-age parenthood have each been the focus of a variety of prevention efforts; however, the connecting link between poverty, adolescent pregnancy, and lack of academic achievement is rarely addressed by coordinated school and community intervention programs. Given the antecedents of pregnancy and school failure, programs need to combine efforts and pay more attention to increasing a teenager's motivation to avoid pregnancy and stay in school. And, conversely, for young women and men to have

Carol Cassell, "Let It Shine: Promoting School Success, Life Aspirations to Prevent School-Aged Parenthood," SIECUS (Sexuality Information and Education Council of the United States) *Report*, vol. 30, no. 3, February–March 2002, p. 7. Copyright 2002 Sexuality Information and Education Council of the U.S., Inc., 130 West 42nd St., Ste. 350, New York, NY 10036, www.siecus.org. Reproduced by permission.

the motivation to avoid involvement in a pregnancy and to succeed in school, they must have concrete options for their futures. . . .

Sophomores . . . with low academic ability were twice as likely to become parents by their senior year as those students with high academic ability.

Studies Link School Failure to Teen Pregnancy

Recent studies have found that two critical problems many adolescents face—pregnancy and school failure—are intertwined. This becomes apparent in the research uncovering the direct correlation between youth that experience school failure and drop out of school and youth at risk for being involved in a pregnancy and school-age parenthood.

Exploring the relationship of academic ability to the potential for teenage parenthood, the High School and Beyond Study [conducted by the National Center for Educational Statistics in the 1980s and 1990s] found that sophomores (both females and males) with low academic ability were twice as likely to become parents by their senior year as those students with high academic ability. Looking at skill levels, the [ongoing] National Longitudinal Survey of Youth found that teen girls in the bottom 20 percent of basic reading and math skills were five times more likely to become mothers over a two-year high school period than those in the top 20 percent.

Although it is common wisdom that the primary reason girls drop out of school is because they are pregnant, recent analyses show that many teen mothers dropped out of school before they got pregnant. A survey of never-married women in their twenties showed that among those who became both pregnant and school dropouts, 61 percent of the pregnancies occurred after dropping out of school; another survey of very young welfare-recipient mothers showed that 20 percent were already out of school before they conceived.

Compounding the problem is that pregnant teens and teen mothers have poor school attendance and experience low levels of academic success. In reviews of antecedents of high-risk behavior related to adolescent pregnancy, students at risk include those with low expectations for school achievement who do not engage in school activities and those with parents who are not supportive or not involved with their child's academic experiences. Moreover, studies show that a sense of limited future educational and job opportunities contribute to a lack of motivation to either practice or use contraceptives effectively.

The link between students' capability to be successful in school and their capacity to avoid school-age pregnancy is further reinforced by the National Study of Adolescent Health (ADD Health) report [a database of the federal government]. The researchers found that adolescents stand a better chance of avoiding risky behavior—including postponing sexual intercourse and pregnancy—when they experience and express strong connections to their school.

Who Are the Mothers?

Although recent statistics demonstrate a decline in both pregnancy and childbearing, the problem of teen pregnancy and parenthood is still of great magnitude. Approximately four in 10 girls become pregnant each year, and there is approximately one birth for every 20 women between 15 and 19 years of age. While most pregnant teens are 18 or 19 years old, approximately 40 percent are 17 or younger. Of the four million babies born each year, one out of eight are born to a teenager, one out of four are born to a mother with less than a high school education, almost one out of three to a mother who lives in poverty, and one out of four to an unmarried mother.

While the current decline in rates is encouraging, a continued decline of adolescent pregnancy and birth rates is not certain. Although the teen birth rate has decreased, the number of births to teens has increased, reflecting an overall increase in the U.S. teen population. Between 2000 and 2010, the number of girls 15 to 19 years of age is estimated to increase by nearly 10 percent. Unless birth rates continue to decrease, the population increase of teen girls may very well mean an increase in teen pregnancies and births.

Understanding the context of teen pregnancy means understanding the impact of pregnancy upon the life of an individual girl and her family. Although the terms *adolescent pregnancy, teenage pregnancy*, and *school-aged parenthood* are usually interchangeably applied to pregnancies among young women in the teen years, the reality is not interchangeable. Pregnancy has vastly different implications for a girl in the developmental stage of early adolescence than for a young woman on the cusp of adulthood.

The experience of pregnancy and the outcomes of childbearing are not the same for the 18- or 19-year-old high school graduate who is married, planning marriage, working, or attending college and for the 13- or 14-year-old student or school dropout. In addition to the economic consequence, a vast majority of young girls under 17 years of age, as appropriate to their development, are biologically and psychologically too immature to raise a child.

Contributing to the cycle of pregnancy, childbearing, and poverty is the way in which adolescents resolve their pregnancies. Young women who come from advantaged families generally have abortions. Childbearing, on the other hand, is concentrated among teenagers who are poor and low income: more than 80 percent of young women who give birth are either poor or low income.

Who Are the Fathers?

There is little information about the young men who father children, an issue complicated by the fact that some of the fathers are out of school or past high school age.

Like teenage mothers, the males who father their children tend to be poor, are often continuing an intergenerational practice (many are from families who experienced teenage childbearing), live in low-income communities, and have low educational achievement. In addition, like early motherhood, early fatherhood appears to have negative consequences of poor school attendance and dropping out of school. Because they obtain less education, these fathers are more likely unemployed, and have lower long-term employment and lower earnings than their counterparts who delay parenthood. . . .

Sexual Abuse, Rape, and Pregnancy

Although the scientific data is sparse, those experienced in working with sexual abuse and rape and those experienced in working with pregnant teens are well aware of the connection between sexual abuse in childhood and pregnancy in adolescence.

It appears that a traumatic underlying cause of teen pregnancy, for many young teenage girls, is that sexual intercourse was involuntary and coerced. The younger a sexually experienced teenage girl is, the more likely she is to have had involuntary sexual intercourse. For example, 74 percent of young women under 13 who have had sexual intercourse reported having had it involuntarily, as compared to 40 percent of girls 15 and under.

Despite realities to the contrary, adolescent parenthood is not always considered a negative among some disadvantaged young women.

A study conducted by the An Ounce of Prevention Fund found that, of the teens who experienced a first pregnancy by age 16, 60 percent reported that they had been forced into an unwanted sexual experience. And a study of teen mothers in Washington State indicated that two thirds were victims of molestation, rape, or attempted rape before their first pregnancy. Forty-four percent of the girls had been raped by age 13.

Disadvantaged Youth View Pregnancy Favorably

Despite realities to the contrary, adolescent parenthood is not always considered a negative among some disadvantaged young women. Having a baby enables the adolescent to enter and become part of a community of young mothers. Parenthood is often the most available marker of success and social power in the face of an otherwise limited life. For these teen mothers, pregnancy and childbirth may be seen as the ticket to achieving an adult status and a sense of independence.

Girls growing up in poverty need to possess not just average but above-average psychological resources and strengths to avoid becoming a pregnant teen.

Not only is it a challenge for young women growing up in poor families to achieve educational competencies and use them effectively, but success in these avenues may uproot them from their families, peers, and neighborhoods. If teenage childbearing is generally acceptable in her family and in her community, it is difficult for a young woman to go against the cultural grain.

For an ambitious young woman, the comfort of belonging is often altered when her education or occupational skills go beyond what her family accepts; and more importantly, what her friends, and especially her male partner, approve of. In a community of high teen pregnancy rates, if a young woman fears being different or isolated from her friends, she may come to believe that having a baby is "no big deal."

Both Teens and Their Children Suffer

Pregnancy and parenting pose major challenges to full-time school attendance. Responsibilities of child-rearing, lack of support from families and peers, and their own immaturity add up to significant barriers for teen parents to stay in school. As a result, adolescent mothers drop out at a staggering rate, and those who have already dropped out are less likely to return to school. Adding to the problem of teen mothers' lack of education is the fact that about 25 percent of them dropped out of school before they became pregnant.

Only about 30 percent of adolescent mothers earn a high school diploma, compared to 76 percent of those who postpone childbearing. Controlling for a wide range of background variables, researchers found that adolescent childbearing alone accounts for more than 40 percent of this difference in graduation rates. . . .

Throughout their school years, the children of adolescent mothers do much worse than the children of older mothers.

Those who grow up in poor, single-parent homes are . . .
2.5 times as likely to become teen mothers.

They are two to three times less likely to be rated "excellent" by their teachers and 50 percent more likely to repeat a grade. And they perform significantly worse on tests of their cognitive development, even after differences in measurable background factors have been screened out.

Rather than declining over time, the educational deficits of children born to adolescent mothers appear to accumulate, causing the child to fall further behind in school as he or she grows older. Only 77 percent of the children of adolescent mothers earn their high school diplomas compared with 89 percent of a comparison group. More than half of the difference is due to these children becoming adolescent parents.

Teen mothers spend more of their young adult years as single parents than do women who delay childbearing, which means that their children spend much of the childhood with only one parent. Being raised by one parent—who is a young teen mother—may cast a long shadow over the lives of many of these children. Compared to their peers growing up with two parents, those who grow up in poor, single-parent homes are twice as likely to drop out of high school, 2.5 times as likely to become teen mothers, and 1.4 times as likely to be out of school and out of work. Even after adjusting for various social and economic differences, children who grow up in single-parent homes have lower grade point averages, lower college aspirations, and poorer school attendance records. . . .

[Teens growing up in poverty] often feel they have nothing to lose by becoming a parent.

Fostering Lifelong Aspirations Will Help

Clearly, a lack of confidence in the future, a sense of limited opportunities, and perception of a life without economic security differentiates school-age parents from those who delay sexual intercourse or use contraceptives consistently.

As many teens growing up in poverty or from working-class poor families do not believe that they have educational or career opportunities, becoming pregnant does not cause the fear of forfeited opportunities that a middle-class teenager perceives.

They often feel they have nothing to lose by becoming a parent; no door will be closed because they believe that no doors are open to them anyway. The belief that there is a positive, attainable future worth planning and preparing for—that there is a future worth having—is the most powerful element in a young person's decision to avoid pregnancy and stay in school.

Based on what we know about the antecedents of school failure and school-age parenthood, communities and schools should engage young people in safe, structured fun and enriching activities focused on building self-worth and self-confidence. Communities can support a wide variety of activities that allow youth to succeed in school: academic, sports, and arts programs; after-school programs such as tutoring and field trips; and mentoring and community service responsibilities.

Simply put, it is adults who pave the way for youth to become successful. We can offer opportunities for young people to be an integral part of school and community life, encourage them to aspire to a rewarding, joyful future, and provide the resources to [ensure] the achievement of their hopes and dreams.

It is imperative that we continue to fund and evaluate programs, such as the ones mentioned above, that combine work on teen pregnancy prevention, youth development, sexuality education, and reproductive health care.

A Father's Absence Contributes to Teen Pregnancy

Ann Quigley

Ann Quigley is a contributing writer to the Health Behavior News Service, which is part of the Washington, D.C.–based Center for the Advancement of Health. The center is an independent nonprofit organization that works to inform the public about the latest research concerning various health issues.

Fathers who leave their families may increase their daughters' risk for early sexual activity and teenage pregnancy, suggest the results of long-term studies in the United States and in New Zealand.

The association between father absence and early teenage sexual activity and pregnancy has long been noted, but many researchers have attributed it to factors associated with divorce, including poverty, family conflict and erosion of parental monitoring. But the new findings suggest a more direct link between a father's absence and his daughter's early teenage sexual activity and pregnancy.

"These findings may support social policies that encourage fathers to form and remain in families with their children," unless there is violence or a high degree of conflict, says study author Bruce J. Ellis of the Department of Psychology at the University of Canterbury in Christchurch, New Zealand.

Father Absence Boosts Risk of Early Pregnancy

Among Western industrialized countries, the United States and New Zealand have the highest and second-highest rates of teenage pregnancy, past research has shown. Teenage childbearing is associated with a host of problems, including lower educational and career achievements, health problems and inadequate social support for parenting.

"Given these costs to adolescents and their children, it is critical to identify life experiences and pathways that place girls at increased risk for early sexual activity and adolescent pregnancy," Ellis says.

Researchers found that father absence places daughters at special risk for early sexual activity and teenage pregnancy.

Ellis and colleagues analyzed data from two long-term studies that followed the progress of 242 girls in the United States and 520 girls in New Zealand for their entire childhoods, from before kindergarten to approximately age 18. Based on multiple interviews and questionnaires administered over the years to both parents and children, the data covered everything from family demographics to parenting styles and child behavioral problems to childhood academic performance.

The researchers defined absence of the biological or adoptive birth father at or before the child reached age 5 as early onset of father absence, while late onset of father absence was defined as occurring when the child was between 6 and 13.

The researchers found that father absence places daughters at special risk for early sexual activity and teenage pregnancy. While the researchers said these findings need to be replicated in non-Western [countries], "the striking similarity in results across the United States and New Zealand samples underscores the robustness and generalizability of the findings," Ellis says.

The study results are published in the [May/June 2003] issue of the journal *Child Development*.

Earlier Exit Increases the Risk

Ellis and colleagues noted that girls whose fathers left the family earlier in their lives had the highest rates of both early sexual activity and adolescent pregnancy, followed by those whose fathers left at a later age, followed by girls whose fathers were present.

"It is not just a matter of whether the father is absent, but the timing of that absence," Ellis says. "This issue may be especially relevant to predicting rates of teenage pregnancy, which were seven to eight times higher among early father-absent girls, but only two to three times higher among later father-absent girls, than among father-present girls."

Even when the researchers took into account other factors that could have contributed to early sexual activity and pregnancy, such as behavioral problems and life adversity, early father-absent girls were still about five times more likely in the United States and three times more likely in New Zealand to experience an adolescent pregnancy than were father-present girls.

Father Absence Is a Strong Indicator

Girls who grew up in otherwise socially and economically privileged homes were not protected. "Father absence was so fundamentally linked to teenage pregnancy that its effects were largely undiminished by such factors as whether girls were rich or poor, black or white, New Zealand Maori [native people] or European, cooperative or defiant in temperament, born to adult or teenage mothers, raised in safe or violent neighborhoods, subjected to few or many stressful life events, reared by supportive or rejecting parents, exposed to functional or dysfunctional marriages, or closely or loosely monitored by parents," Ellis says.

The researchers suggested several mechanisms to explain the results. One is that a longer duration of father absence results in the daughters having greater exposure to their mothers' dating and future relationship behaviors, and this exposure may encourage earlier onset of sexual behavior in daughters. Another possibility is that girls who experience father absence may undergo early personality changes that orient them toward early and unstable bonds with men.

One study weakness is that it could not identify possible genetic causes for the findings, say the study authors. For example, fathers whose inherited temperaments predispose them toward aggression, disruption and resistance to control may be more likely to abandon their families. Daughters who inherit such traits may be more likely to engage in early sexual activity.

Sexual Abuse Contributes to Teen Pregnancy

Joanna Lipper

Joanna Lipper is a Harvard-trained filmmaker and author who runs Sea Wall Entertainment, a company that develops and produces books and films. Her book Growing Up Fast *grew out of a documentary film with the same title.*

Statistics show that a significant number of teen mothers . . . have painful histories indelibly marked by sexual trauma. In July 1998 the *Journal of the American Medical Association* published a review of several of the most conclusive research studies to date regarding the significant links between sexual abuse and teen pregnancy:

> Child and adolescent sexual abuse is a risk factor for teen pregnancy on two levels. First, sexual abuse is a common antecedent of adolescent pregnancy, with up to 66% of pregnant teens reporting histories of abuse. Conversely, sexually abused adolescent girls are significantly more likely to have been pregnant than teens without abuse histories. A history of sexual abuse has been linked to high-risk behaviors that may account for increased risk of early unplanned pregnancy, including young age at initiation of sexual intercourse, failure to use contraception, prostitution, engagement in relationships involving physical assault, and abuse of alcohol and other drugs. Moreover, girls with histories of sexual abuse have been found to have a greater desire to conceive and increased concerns about infertility than girls without abuse histories.

Abuse Is Linked to Teen Pregnancy

At age eight, Liz [a teen mom interviewed by the author] found a way to tell the story of her molestation to a judge, but how many young girls and teenagers remain silent, repressing, suffering, and disassociating as the abuse goes on, sometimes for years. . . . How many doctors neglect to ask pregnant teenagers if they have ever been sexually abused? Every day in this country, how many sex education classes are taught in which the phrase *sexual abuse* is never even mentioned? Can sex education classes that promote "abstinence only" give teenagers and preteens the knowledge, comfort level, and negotiation skills to defend themselves against molestation, incest, date rape, and sex described as "voluntary but not really wanted"?

For years a cloak of silence, denial, and discomfort has covered sexual abuse in medical and educational settings and within American society at large, preventing the public from clearly seeing key factors that are inextricably entwined with the roots of teen pregnancy. The scandal within the Catholic Church [in which priests have been accused of molesting children] has opened up a dialogue about sexual abuse, but perhaps even more difficult for society to stomach is the thought of sexual abuse occurring with alarming frequency within the four walls of the family home. Without widespread acknowledgment of the prevalence of childhood sexual abuse in all its forms and a strategy to address this particular risk factor, plans for significantly reducing teen pregnancy remain incomplete, like a puzzle missing a crucial, central piece.

Abused Girls Are Less Likely to Protect Themselves

After years of experience counseling teen mothers, Joann Oliver accepted the position of clinical coordinator at Berkshire County Kids' Place, a child-advocacy center in Pittsfield [Massachusetts] that specializes in treating children who have disclosed sexual abuse. . . .

One of the biggest challenges Joann faces in her job is explaining the family dynamics within which sexual abuse occurs. Often these dynamics are either not well known or are misunderstood.

"We're often asked by the police or the D.A.'s [district attorney's] office, 'Why didn't this kid tell, if the abuse has been going on for five years?' I have to explain that maybe a young girl didn't disclose because the perpetrator said that her family would fall apart and her mother would kick her out. And, in fact, when she does tell, that's exactly what happens."

. . .

"In households where there's sexual abuse and/or domestic violence, there are not good boundaries in place," Joann explained. "There's a lot of sexual innuendo and a lot of situations where boundaries just are not defined. If a young girl is in the bathroom taking a shower and her father or stepfather or brother comes in to go to the bathroom, even if they don't look at her, they are showing no regard for boundaries and no respect for her space.

"Then when these girls grow up and they end up in a relationship where the other person is possessive and likes to know where they're going and what they're doing all the time, they actually see that as loving and caring rather than as controlling. They often think, 'Oh, this person cares so much about me. He doesn't want me to see my friends, he only wants me to be with him.' I don't even think these young women see their bodies as their own. They find love by physical contact and they end up in these relationships where they're not able to say, 'Stop!' or, 'We need to use protection!'"

Self-Destructive Behavior Follows Abuse

Over the years, Joann has closely observed and documented the symptoms exhibited by teenagers who have been sexually abused. Suffering immensely, these troubled adolescents often engaged in high-risk, self-destructive behaviors such as self-cutting, drug use, excessive drinking, promiscuity, and running away. As Joann astutely pointed out, these symptoms were identical to the high-risk behaviors that resulted in their getting into situations in which they faced a huge risk of getting pregnant. When Liz ran away at thirteen to escape her abusive, promiscuous mother and the host of boyfriends drifting in and out of the family home, she subsequently sought food and shelter in the apartments of adult men who were able to convince her that they "loved" her.

Joann has seen numerous cases . . . in which adolescents' accounts of intolerable home situations were contradicted by their parents and simply not believed by the Department of Social Services or the police, resulting in the teenagers being shuttled from one foster home to another in between repetitious stints in their original malignant home environments.

"A lot of the struggles we have with the different professions and agencies we have to work with relate to the problem that sometimes the high-risk self-destructive behaviors ruin the girl's credibility," explained Joann, "so then when she comes forward and says that she has been sexually abused, oftentimes a parent or family member may say, 'Well, she's always running away, or she's always lying to me. Now she's lying about this, too.' It's a double-edged sword because the very symptoms that are due to the sexual abuse often confuse people into thinking that the girl is not credible.

"Most of the time if a child or teen discloses and the mother does not support them or believe them, the chances of them recanting are pretty high," said Joann. "We've had a number of cases with teen girls where they've disclosed and the perpetrator has been the mother's boyfriend or their stepfather. What happens then is that the mother doesn't believe the girl partly because of those acting-out behaviors I spoke about earlier. So she's forced to make a decision to kick the father out or to put the child in foster care. Oftentimes the girl goes to foster care and the mom continues living with the perpetrator. In those situations, those girls are at a much higher risk for teen parenthood."

Having a Sibling Who Is a Teen Parent Contributes to Teen Pregnancy

National Campaign to Prevent Teen Pregnancy

Founded in 1996, the National Campaign to Prevent Teen Pregnancy is a nonprofit, nonpartisan organization that seeks to improve the lives of children, youth, and their families by reducing teen pregnancy. The organization does this by bringing awareness to the issue on the national level as well as providing assistance and resources to those already working on the issue.

According to several studies, younger siblings of teen parents are *2 to 6 times* more likely to become pregnant as teens than younger siblings of teens who are not parents. Younger siblings of teen parents also are more likely to be sexually active during early adolescence than teens whose older siblings are not teen parents.

For example, one study found that 50% of younger siblings of teen parents were sexually active, compared to 24% of those whose older siblings were not teen parents. Another study concluded that, "having an adolescent childbearing sister has a stronger effect on permissive sexual attitudes and non-virgin status than does having many sexually active sisters."

Teen Parents Have an Influence on Siblings

Two studies take an interesting approach to analyzing the effect of having an older sibling teen parent. The first study looked at the effect of having multiple teen parents in the family. It found that 23% of younger sisters with two or more teen-parenting sisters were sexually experienced, compared to

National Campaign to Prevent Teen Pregnancy, "Younger Siblings of Teen Parents: At Increased Risk of Teen Pregnancy?" December 2004. Reproduced by permission.

16% of younger sisters with only one teen-parenting sister. Among younger brothers of three or more teen-parenting sisters, 27% were sexually experienced compared to 17% of younger brothers with one or two teen-parenting sisters.

Younger siblings of teen parents ... seem to have more accepting attitudes towards early sex and teenage pregnancy.

The second study divided the comparison group of teens with non-parenting siblings into two groups: those whose older sister had *never* been pregnant and those whose older sister had been pregnant, but did not give birth. The study found that younger sisters with a teen-parenting older sister were more likely to be teen parents themselves (51%) than younger sisters of teens that had never been pregnant (44%).

Permissive Attitudes Prevail

Younger siblings of teen parents also seem to have more accepting attitudes towards early sex and teenage pregnancy compared to youth whose older siblings are not parents. Younger girls living with two or more sibling teen parents tend to have even more permissive sexual and childbearing attitudes than those only living with one teen parent, and they are more likely to say that they intend to become sexually active and have a child in the near future. In addition, younger siblings of teen parents tend to have lower educational aspirations and more problems at school than siblings of non-parenting teens. Both characteristics—lower education aspirations and problems at school—are associated with increased risk of early sexual activity and pregnancy. The risk of school problems also increases with the number of teen-parenting siblings in the family. Other risk factors for early sex that appear to be more prevalent in younger siblings of teen parents include participating in delinquent behavior and being around peers who are sexually active.

Why Are Younger Siblings at Risk?

The fact that younger siblings of teen parents are at increased risk of early sex and pregnancy may seem counterintuitive. These teens see firsthand the hardships of being a teen parent and should have less romanticized views of babies and parenting, all of which would hypothetically motivate them to avoid becoming teen parents themselves. On the other hand, as discussed below, there are many reasons why having an older sibling who is a teen parent might increase the risk.

One possibility is shared risk factors. Dozens of characteristics, both of the teens and of their environment, have been identified as increasing the risk of early sex and pregnancy. Characteristics related to teens' environments and the people in their lives are likely to affect *all* children in a family. For example, if one teen's risk of pregnancy is partially due to living in poverty, in a single parent family, or in an unsafe neighborhood, these factors will similarly increase pregnancy risk among the younger siblings living in the same household.

The studies discussed above controlled for some of these risk factors, including age and pubertal status of the teen, gender, race/ethnicity, family size and type, socioeconomic status and receipt of welfare, parental education, and whether teens lived in an urban environment. However, other factors were not controlled for, so some of the increased risk may be due to shared background characteristics.

Modeling Plays a Role

Another theory is that teen parents affect siblings through modeling. Many teen pregnancy prevention programs are based on [Albert] Bandura's Social Learning Theory, which holds that individuals can learn new behavior (such as refusal skills or negotiation over contraceptive use) by observing the behavior of others. Here, however, younger siblings may be learning negative behavior modeled by their older siblings. Siblings' relationships also may result in the transfer of permissive attitudes toward early sex and pregnancy, since younger siblings often look up to their older siblings for advice, support and guidance in these areas.

Younger sisters who perceive that their parents favor their older pregnant/parenting sibling are likely to mimic their older siblings' behavior.

Two studies have considered these factors. One found that younger sisters of teen mothers who reported a close relationship with their sister were more likely to have permissive attitudes toward childbearing than those whose relationships with their older sisters were less close. However, the second study found that a positive relationship between siblings actually increased the younger sisters' educational aspirations and had no significant effects on sexual behavior or attitudes.

Most teen parents also model school failure—for example, 59% of teen mothers under age 18 drop out of high school. This may help explain why younger siblings of teen parents have more negative attitudes and expectations regarding school and career, compared to those whose older siblings are not teen parents.

Family Dynamics Play a Role

Some younger siblings feel threatened about their place in the family when an older sibling becomes a teen parent. Younger sisters who perceive that their parents favor their older pregnant/parenting sibling are likely to mimic their older siblings' behavior. Studies also have found that when extensive rivalry or jealousy exists between a teen mother and her younger sibling, the latter is more likely to engage in problem behaviors and be sexually experienced.

One study found that the average younger sibling of a teen parent spent more than 10 hours a week caring for the child. In fact, the more time a younger sister spent in child care activities, the more likely she was to have pessimistic school aspirations, be sexually active, and to intend to have a child right away. Among younger brothers, however, time spent in child care activities either had no effects or was associated with more negative views toward early childbearing.

Parents of Teen Parents Play a Role

Another theory about why younger siblings of teen parents are more likely to become teen parents themselves is that parenting styles change after a teenage daughter gives birth. One study found that parental monitoring of all children in a family decreased after one child becomes a teen parent. This may be, in part, because parents end up spending considerable time caring for the grandchild—an average of 30 hours per week, according to one study.

Some parents may view their child becoming a teen parent as their own failure and may feel incapable of affecting their other children's sexual behavior. These feelings may extend beyond their children's sexual behavior—parents of teen parents also often have lower educational and career expectations for all their children than parents whose children have not given birth.

Mothers of teen parents were found to be less affectionate and more critical with all their children than mothers of non-childbearing teens, especially when the family was experiencing economic hardship or the mother spent many hours caring for the grandchild. . . .

Programs Should Target Younger Siblings

When it comes to sibling's risk of teen pregnancy, there is still much to learn. For instance, it would be helpful to know if other programs exist that include a prevention component specifically for siblings of teen parents and, if so, whether they are effective and what makes them effective. Regarding teen parents' influence on their younger siblings, more information on the effects of gender, age differences, and relationship quality would be informative.

Even with the paucity of existing research on the topic, what is known clearly indicates that younger siblings of teen parents are important targets for prevention efforts because they are at increased risk for becoming teen parents themselves. Efforts, attention, and resources should be allocated accordingly.

Society's Growing Acceptance of Teen Pregnancy Contributes to the Phenomenon

Vikki Ortiz

Vikki Ortiz is a pop culture and features writer for the Milwaukee Journal Sentinel.

The final bell of the day rings at Lady Pitts high school [in Milwaukee], and 100 girls slowly wander out of their classrooms to discover a surprise.

Long, rectangular tables covered with plastic cloths have been set up along the school's only hallway. Submarine sandwiches, cups of punch, cake and baby gifts are on each of the tables. Delighted, the teen moms fall into line.

Such is the current approach to teen pregnancy.

Overly Accepting Attitudes Pose a Problem

Decades ago, young girls were forced to leave high school for getting pregnant, and teen parents struggled to get help. Today, two Milwaukee public high schools have day care centers. Parenting skills are taught to teens at city and suburban hospitals, community centers and schools. And those 100 girls at Lady Pitts? They were given little blankets and baby clothes from a local sorority as part of "Finer Womanhood" month.

Few people would argue for a return to the days of ostracism. But some people who work closely with teens now wonder whether the accepting attitude toward teen pregnancy that evolved in the last quarter-century is actually contributing to the phenomenon.

Milwaukee has the second-highest rate of teen pregnancy of major cities in the country after Baltimore—and it's been at or near the top of the list for many years. In some suburbs, although the count is much lower than in the city, the number of teen births has doubled or almost tripled in the last decade, according to the state Department of Health and Family Services.

Studies show that the vast majority of teen moms are not married, have not graduated from high school and have not settled into a job.

That says a lot about not just Milwaukee's past and present, but also its future, because a cycle has been created, says Ken Little, former president of the Milwaukee Urban League. Today, Milwaukee is paying for the high number of pregnant teens from decades ago with high numbers of impoverished, uneducated and unskilled parents. Little says that if we, as a community, do not teach teen parents a different way of thinking—Milwaukee will continue to pay, as this generation of children born to teens grows up and has children while themselves in their teens.

"If you see a problem and you don't fix it, then it continues to get worse," Little says.

Acceptance vs. Support

Studies show that the vast majority of teen moms are not married, have not graduated from high school and have not settled into a job. Many get no support from the babies' fathers, who very likely also don't have solid employment or much of a future. Their children are less likely to obtain what the Annie E. Casey Foundation, a leader in children's issues, calls "the emotional and financial resources they need to develop into independent, productive, well-adjusted adults."

The trick, then, is negotiating the fine line of offering support for teens facing parenthood without condoning the situation.

"What happened to the moral upbringing of our children, with family values and supervision?" asks Don Krueger, retired principal of [Milwaukee] South Division High School. "Anything goes. Right now, anything goes."

Krueger thinks the whole community needs a wake-up call. Schools, churches and the law need to collaborate on a message that says premarital sex and teen pregnancy happen, but shouldn't. And yes, there are services available, but they should be to help, not to condone.

"It's a huge dilemma," says Susan Sikora, director of family programs at Rosalie Manor, which runs "Supporting Today's Parents," a program that offers first-time parents advice, parenting lessons, nursing and other services at almost every hospital in Milwaukee County. "I just don't think there's a quick answer. I think we keep doing what we've been doing."

. . .

A Tale of Numbers

In 1970, the birth rate for females ages 15 to 19 in the city of Milwaukee was 59 per 1,000. The number climbed to 75.6 per 1,000 in 1980 and then to 94 per 1,000 in 1985. At that point, the city made national headlines for having the nation's highest rate of births among black teens, reporting that out of 3,953 births to black women, 1,175, or 29.7%, were to teens. State health officials demanded that more money and programs be dedicated to the teen pregnancy problem. A few years later, one north side alderwoman [city government elected representative] was so exasperated she actually suggested sterilization as a way to keep the city's teen pregnancy rate under control.

Yet even with the added attention, teen pregnancies continued to rise. By 1990, the Milwaukee Health Department reported the birth rate for females ages 15 to 19 at 117.8 per 1,000.

The numbers finally began to dip in the 1990s. In 1995, the teen birth rate was 106 per 1,000, and by 2000, the rate was down to 89.5 per 1,000. That's still nearly double the national teen birth rate of 50 per 1,000. . . .

Many Teens Unfazed by Pregnancy

As retired principal of South Division High School, Krueger sees his students come to class pleased about expecting a baby. He talks to their parents, who tell him they are proud of their children, proud about the grandchildren on the way.

[Some teens] are genuinely disappointed when pregnancy tests turn up negative.

Krueger sees students who deliver children without even reporting the pregnancies to school officials, registering for parenting classes or getting versed on financial assistance.

Isn't there something wrong, Krueger wonders, when he tells a pregnant girl: "That guy isn't going to be there" for her, and the girl answers: "Yeah, I know that," without a trace of concern.

"They think that everything is going to be just fine, and it just breaks my heart to see the hard, hard life they have prepared for themselves," Krueger says.

Pregnancy Is Viewed as a Normal Occurrence

Of course, not all teens exhibit this attitude. At some high schools, teen pregnancy is still a rarity and a shock to the student population. Sexual activity may not be part of some students' worlds at all.

Still, Carol Wantuch, public health officer for the suburb of Cudahy, says she is amazed to see so many teens accept pregnancy as a matter of fact. And then there are those who are genuinely disappointed when pregnancy tests turn up negative.

"Across the board, it's OK to be single and pregnant," Wantuch says. "Everybody is going to 'ooh and ah' over the baby."

Teen Moms Are Getting Younger

Teen pregnancy is not limited to high school students, either.

[In 2002], Milwaukee Public Schools [opened] the district's first charter school aimed at reaching middle school-age parents, something incomprehensible a generation ago.

The idea for the school came after Valerie Benton-Davis, [a Milwaukee Public Schools] teacher for 10 years, noticed a number of middle school students getting pregnant. In December [2001], Benton-Davis made a somewhat radical proposal to the Milwaukee School Board: Northern Star School would be aimed at reaching "at-risk" children, which in most cases would mean teen parents, ages 11 to 14, at risk of not graduating.

Some [teens] describe sex as a hobby, a pastime, a sport. Others describe it as an obligation, proof of commitment to their partners.

The presentation seemed to strike a chord with School Board members. The school [was] scheduled to open with at least 60 students.

The school's main objective [is] to keep the students on track toward graduation. If that is not possible, school officials hope to at least give the adolescents skills that will make them employable, so they can support their families.

"Obviously the problem is not going to go away, because it still exists," says Benton-Davis. "I think offering an academic program that can meet the needs of school-age parents can help them be successful for the future."

Breaking the Cycle

The school's biggest challenge, Benton-Davis says, will be trying to get the students to understand that the cycle of teen pregnancy needs to stop with them.

Many of today's school-age parents are the products of teen pregnancies themselves—their parents are the ones who pushed Milwaukee up the national charts. They grew up thinking it was normal; they wouldn't envision themselves doing anything differently—like going to college, Benton-Davis says.

Listening to some of those students can be a quick lesson in how comfortable teens have become with the notion of having children. Some describe sex as a hobby, a pastime, a sport. Others describe it as an obligation, proof of commitment to their partners. Still others describe it as a rite of passage into adulthood.

Ask a few of them about the "teen pregnancy problem" and they're confused. They're aware that teen pregnancy is an issue, but they never thought of it as a problem.

Pregnancy Viewed as a Positive Step Forward

Lakisha Rollins of Milwaukee will say that she loved Ernest Clay. They grew up together in Clarksville, Miss., and became a couple [in 2000], when she was 14. For the first year of their relationship, they used condoms, because they weren't sure where their futures were headed. But by the second year together, they decided they didn't need protection.

When Rollins started eating more and her shape started changing, her mother accused her of being pregnant. She denied it. Then she and her boyfriend went to a medical clinic, and she took a pregnancy test. It was positive.

"I wasn't upset. I was happy, but then again, I was scared because I wasn't sure how people were going to react to me," Rollins says.

To Rollins, being pregnant gave her future some definition. It made her feel as if she was going to be with her boyfriend for the rest of their lives.

"A lot of people were going through that, and they were together," Rollins says.

School-Age Parenting Changes Life

For much of the pregnancy, Rollins stayed in Clarksville with her mother, who told her daughter she was disappointed but "there was nothing she could do because it happened." When Rollins' mother died suddenly of a brain aneurysm about six months into the pregnancy, Rollins left Clay and moved to Milwaukee to live with her older sister, Linda Rollins.

On Jan. 15, 2001, Rollins was holding a bowl of macaroni in her sister's dining room when she felt an intense pressure in her stomach. Her brother-in-law drove her to the hospital, and her sister kept her company through the labor pains, which lasted two hours. When it came time to deliver, Linda Rollins left the room and Lakisha gave birth to a girl, whom she named Kandi.

Two days after Kandi's birth, Lakisha Rollins called Clay. His mother answered. She told Rollins that Clay had been put in jail for carrying a concealed weapon. He would be behind bars for the next year and a half.

Rollins now says she does not count on a life with Clay. She wants to concentrate on finishing school and getting a job. The baby, she says, keeps her off the streets.

"I felt like by me having a child, I needed to be doing good," Rollins says. "I tried to make a change, make something different about me."

Teens Say Pregnancy Is Not a Problem

Kandi goes to day care as her mother continues school at Lady Pitts, a school for pregnant teens and teen mothers operated out of a wing at Custer High School. After school, Rollins' sister takes the baby from day care and stays with her as Rollins works at a local company tutoring little kids on the computer. Rollins rejoins her daughter after work, in the early evening.

Rollins claims she has a plan: to graduate from high school and then take a few months off before going to Jackson State University in Jackson, Miss. She says her brother, who lives in her home state, has already agreed to take care of the baby when she goes to college.

In the meantime, she makes use of some of the resources available to teen mothers. Each month, Rosalie Manor sends her a letter, spelling out the various developments her daughter should have for that age. She also has attended several lectures by the Milwaukee Urban League, which pays her $25 for each session on topics such as the importance of school and getting along with parents.

Does Rollins think the number of teen mothers will ever drop significantly?

Teens like her "don't look at it as a problem," Rollins says. "It's the way of life."

Support Programs Are Necessary

Studies indicate that 68% of high schoolers in the United States will have had sex before they graduate. The average age at which a boy loses his virginity is 16.8; the average age for a girl, 17.4.

But don't tell that to Kristin Herns. An 18-year-old Milwaukee mother of two, she doesn't know if any of the efforts being put forth will ever curb attitudes toward sex and having babies.

"Most of the people do it. If you put 100 kids in a line, at least 80 of those kids are having sex," Herns claims, adding that she thinks the average kid becomes sexually active at 10 years old.

For her, a baby shower like the one thrown at Lady Pitts, where she goes to school, is the realistic way to deal with teen pregnancy. Young girls already know their lives are significantly changed because they've had babies. A shower is a form of much-needed support, she says.

This was the intention of members of the local Zeta Phi Beta sorority, which organized the shower, a first for Lady Pitts. Members of the sorority saw the party as a way to encourage the young girls to stay positive about their futures.

"They need to know that having a baby doesn't end their lives. They need to pick themselves up by the bootstraps and keep on going," said Brenda Reed, president of Zeta Phi Beta.

Support Programs Are Flourishing

Since 1995, the Milwaukee Adolescent Pregnancy Prevention Consortium has worked with more than 150 agencies on the issue. The idea behind the consortium is to unite churches, schools and community groups to get the message out about avoiding pregnancy. The group is behind all those "Express Love Without Sex" posters and billboards around the Milwaukee area.

Today, even Catholic high schools participate in teen parenting classes.

Many of the agencies participating in the consortium have grown dramatically through the years.

Rosalie Manor, where Sikora works, is one example. Back in 1988, the organization had a budget of $300,000 for its Supporting Today's Parents program, money that came from Milwaukee County and matching private grant funds. Then, workers visited two hospitals in the area, meeting with first-time parents, Sikora says.

By 1992—when the city of Milwaukee had some of the highest teen pregnancy numbers in its history—the program's budget had doubled to $600,000, and services began being offered at six area hospitals.

Today, the program has a budget of a little more than $1.5 million, and first-time parents are being reached at every delivery hospital in Milwaukee County, except for West Allis Memorial, which has its own program for teen parents. Those reached by Rosalie Manor will, at the very least, be given a packet of information listing resources available to parents, and follow-up informational letters.

Other young parents will be given free home nursing visits, social work services and parenting skills lessons through Rosalie Manor or the different agencies it works with, Sikora says.

These Days Pregnant Teens Blend In

When [June] Martin-Perry, of New Concept Self-Development Center, looks at how far the area has come in addressing teen pregnancy, she is amazed. When New Concept started [to provide pregnancy prevention programs] in 1985, there were limits to whom the center would reach, and few other programs for teenage parents were out there.

Today, even Catholic high schools participate in teen parenting classes.

"I think the acceptance and the changing of norms have made it easier for girls to blend into society," Martin-Perry says. "You used to be appalled when you saw a young girl who was pregnant. But now, it's just like, 'There's another girl who's pregnant.'"

Many Factors Contribute to Teen Pregnancy

Martin Donohoe

Martin Donohoe is an assistant clinical professor of medicine at Oregon Health and Science University. He is also affiliated with the Center for Ethics in Health Care.

The subject of teen pregnancy is frequently covered in major newspapers and magazines. The impression made by dramatic headlines is one of irresponsible, sex-crazed young people engaging in promiscuous, unprotected sex leading to an "epidemic" of teen pregnancies. These articles, as well as current government, insurance industry, and educational policies related to teen pregnancy, often ignore sound science and public health and are marred by misinformation, religious zealotry, simplistic and unworkable solutions, and prejudice and "victim blaming."

Teen Pregnancy Rates Are Decreasing

Greater than 50 percent of high school-age adolescents are sexually active; average age at first intercourse is 17 for girls and 16 for boys. Current birth rates of girls age 15 to 19 (49 births per thousand females) have gradually decreased since 1960. Over the last ten years [from 1993 to 2003], the percentage of high school students who have had multiple partners decreased by 24 percent. Up to two-thirds of adolescents use condoms, three times as many as did so in the 1970s.

Teen Pregnancy Is Linked to Poverty

Despite the increased use of birth control, the U.S. has rates of teen pregnancy which are three to ten times higher than those

Martin Donohoe, "Teen Pregnancy," *Z Magazine*, vol. 16, no. 4, April 2003, pp. 14–16. Reproduced by permission of the author.

among the industrialized nations of Western Europe. U.S. teen poverty rates are higher by a similar magnitude. Six out of seven U.S. teen births are to the 40 percent of girls living at or below the poverty level, and more teenage girls are dropping below this level due to Clinton/Bush [federal government] policies aimed at "reforming" (deforming?) welfare.

Adult Males Usually Impregnate Teenage Girls

The role of adult males in teen pregnancy is under-recognized. In the most comprehensive study to date of males directly responsible for teen pregnancies, conducted in California in 1993, 71 percent of teen pregnancies (for whom a father was reported) were fathered by adult men with an average age of 22.6 years, or 5 years older than the mothers. More births were fathered by men over 25 than by boys under 18. Sexually transmitted disease and acquired immunodeficiency syndrome rates among teenage girls are two to four times higher than among age-matched teenage boys; instead, teenage girls' rates are closer to adult male rates. Statutory rape, in which adult perpetrators or boyfriends have sexual intercourse with under-age girls, is infrequently reported by providers. States are evenly split on whether or not mandated reporting is required.

Lack of Access to Contraception Facilitates Teen Pregnancy

Only 8 percent of U.S. high schools provide condoms, despite the fact that promotion and distribution of condoms does not increase teen sexual activity. Access to contraception of all types is particularly burdensome for rural teens. Recently, legislation that would prohibit prescribed contraceptives for adolescents without parental involvement was introduced in ten states and the U.S. Congress. A survey of girls younger than 18 seeking services at Planned Parenthood found that mandatory notification for prescribed contraceptives would impede girls' use of sexual health care services, potentially increasing teen pregnancies and the spread of STDs [sexually transmitted diseases].

The vast majority of sex education programs in the U.S. do not affect teenage behavior in any substantial way.

Across the U.S., many health plans fail to cover all contraceptive methods, even though all methods are more effective and less costly than no method. Many fewer plans cover abortion than cover sterilization, leaving poor women in the unenviable position of having to choose sterilization if they lack the resources for adequate contraception or for an abortion (which may become necessary even when accepted contraceptive methods are used as directed). . . .

The availability of emergency contraception should help further decrease teen pregnancy rates, especially if it becomes available over-the-counter, as the American Medical Association and the American College of Obstetrics and Gynecology have recommended. Even so, some Catholic hospitals prohibit discussion of emergency contraception, even with rape victims.

Sex Education Is Often Ineffective

The vast majority of sex education programs in the U.S. do not affect teenage behavior in any substantial way. They neither promote more sexual activity, nor do they significantly reduce unprotected sex. The few programs that do work give teenagers a clear and narrow message—delay having sex, but if you have sex, always use a condom. Good programs also teach teens how to resist peer pressure. Unfortunately, "Welfare Reform" legislation allocated states $50 million over 5 years to teach abstinence, rather than to provide contraceptives. In 1988, only 2 percent of U.S. school districts relied solely on abstinence-only sex education programs; by 1999, 23 percent did.

Abortions Are Increasingly Difficult to Obtain

Contrary to occasional media depictions of teens as the main recipients of abortions, 48 percent of those having the procedure are over age 25; 20 percent are married; 56 percent have children. By age 45, the average female will have had 1.4 unintended pregnancies; 43 percent will have had an induced abortion. Fifty-eight percent of women with unintended pregnancies get pregnant while using birth control. This is not surprising, given one year contraceptive failure rates ranging from 2 to 3 percent for IUDs [intrauterine devices], to 7 percent for contraceptive pills, to 21 percent for periodic abstinence. Even so, between 1990 and 2000, the number of annual abortions dropped 18 percent, from 1.6 million to 1.3 million.

Since the 1973 *Roe v. Wade* decision legalizing abortion, various barriers have been erected in the path of those seeking to obtain one. The Hyde Amendment of 1977 cut off Medicaid funding for nearly all abortions. Before former President Clinton took office [in 1993], discussion of abortion in federally funded health clinics was prohibited. Thirty-nine states have parental notification laws, which have led to a rise in late trimester abortions and to increased numbers of abortions in neighboring states without such laws. . . .

Obstacles to abortion include bans on specific methods, mandated waiting periods, [and] parental and spousal notification laws.

The [George W.] Bush administration drafted a policy that would let states define unborn children as persons eligible for medical coverage. The [same] Administration has also introduced bills to increase the $3 million per year already spent on so-called "Crisis Pregnancy Centers," in which pregnant women are given non-factual information regarding abortion, refused information about contraception, shown an ultrasound of their fetus, and watch a slide show depicting bloody aborted fetuses in which it is claimed that abortion is a leading cause of sterility, deformed children and death. In fact, it is 30 times more dangerous to carry a fetus to term than to undergo a legal abortion. The availability of mifepristone (RU-486) for medical pregnancy termination has the potential to improve women's access to safe abortion.

Abortion Costs Are Rarely Covered by Insurance

Abortions cost approximately $350; most patients pay out of pocket. Only one out of three patients has insurance coverage, and only one out of three insurance companies cover the procedure after the deductible is met. Thirty-four states provide no Medicaid funding for abortion; of the 16 that provide coverage, most make it available only in cases of fetal abnormality, rape, or when the pregnant woman's life is endangered or health at risk because of the pregnancy. Often patients are reluctant to file claims due to confidentiality concerns.

Other obstacles to abortion include bans on specific methods, mandated waiting periods, parental and spousal notification laws, regulation of abortion facility locations, zoning ordinances designed to keep abortion clinics from being built in certain areas, and TRAP (Targeted Regulation of Abortion Providers) laws.

Bills already approved by the House of Representatives, and headed for the Republican-majority Senate, include: the Unborn Victims of Violence Act, which gives legal status to a fetus hurt or killed during the commission of a federal crime [this became a law in 2004]; the Child Custody Protection Act, which makes it a crime in some cases to transport a minor across state lines for an abortion [reinforced in 2005]; and the Abortion Non-Discrimination Act, forbidding state and local government actions against hospitals or health care workers who refuse to participate in abortions [signed into law in 2004]. Three recent appointments to the Food and Drug Administration's Reproductive Health Drugs Advisory Committee, Drs. David Hager, Susan Crockett and Joseph Stanford, are avowed foes of abortion rights. Obstetrician-gynecologist Hager, who has advocated Scripture reading and prayer for premenstrual syndrome, reportedly refuses to provide contraceptives to unmarried women.

Practical Policies Will Reduce Teen Pregnancy

It is time to approach teen pregnancy with rational public health policies, which acknowledge the myriad social injustices facilitating teen pregnancy, employ methods known to reduce unwanted pregnancies, and aim to improve the health and welfare of teenage mothers and their children. Suggested policies could include:

- Early, ongoing, and accurate sex education

- Enhanced access to reproductive health services, through the enactment of universal coverage and by building, staffing, and providing protection for the staff of reproductive health clinics

- More comprehensive training of physicians, especially obstetrician-gynecologists, in contraception and abortion

- Overturning parental notification laws; increasing federal funding for family planning

- Providing financial and other incentives to support young women who wish to continue their education and to improve the lives of those living in poverty (for example, via enactment of living wage statutes and by bringing women's salaries into line with those of men having equivalent training and job requirements).

Success in these endeavors will require the concerted efforts of medical educators, health professionals, teachers, employers, non-governmental organizations, concerned citizens, and our elected representatives.

Current
CONTROVERSIES

CHAPTER 3

Do Sex Education Programs Effectively Address Teen Pregnancy?

Chapter Preface

Sex education programs have aroused suspicion and contention since arriving in public schools in the early twentieth century. The debate began around 1913 when Chicago's public schools introduced the nation's first formal sex education program. Billed as a sex hygiene program, it was aimed at curbing the city's growing venereal disease problem, which was spurred on by its thriving red-light districts where prostitution thrived. Since then the disputes have continued as sex education advocates and conservatives spar over the merits and content of such programs.

In his book *Teaching Sex: The Shaping of Adolescence in the 20th Century* Jeffrey P. Moran discusses the history of sex education and highlights the Chicago battle. At the time many people were opposed to the program. While some realized the value of teaching adolescents about sex before they learned it from unscrupulous sources, they did not know if it could be taught without inciting such behavior. It is a question that is still raised by many opponents of sex education.

Moran also notes how the material taught in sex education programs has varied over the years and shifts to conform with the prevailing attitudes of the day. For instance, at one time boys were taught that masturbation damaged their bodies. Later, when adult sexuality was no longer seen as taboo, sex education programs began to include courtship lessons and instruction on human relationships. One aspect, however, has remained consistent—the programs have always suggested that sex is for married people.

During World War II there was another shift as health policy makers worried about soldiers bringing back venereal diseases. Schools stepped up their sexual hygiene programs by exposing students to vivid films and illustrations depicting what would happen to their bodies if they contracted a venereal disease.

During the 1960s the sexual revolution became a driving force in shaping sex education programs. Organizations such as the Sex Information and Education Council of the United States (SIECUS) called for schools to take a scientific approach to sex education and teach responsible sex and sexuality. A backlash followed, and for the next two decades conservative groups rallied for a total ban on sex education. Groups such as the far-right Christian Crusade said sex education programs were nothing more than smut. The Eagle Forum, led by antifeminist Phyllis Schlafly, claimed that sex education stimulated sexual activity among teenagers.

Nonetheless, sex education programs flourished as policy makers, worried about the rising teen pregnancy rate, continued to endorse the programs. By the mid-1980s many schools included sex education as part of their family-life education programs or as part of human development. Besides covering contraception, instruction was given on family finances and parenting skills. These programs also stressed self-esteem and responsibility.

When the AIDS epidemic hit in the 1980s, many policy makers—including U.S. surgeon general C. Everett Koop—called for comprehensive sex education to teach adolescents about condoms and contraceptives so they could protect themselves from AIDS. Many Americans agreed that sex education was imperative. At this time conservative groups gave up on their demands for a ban on sex education and instead began promoting abstinence-only programs.

In his book Moran concludes that the problem with sex educators is that they tend to confuse moral issues with matters of health and illness. This struggle continues today. The authors in this chapter take a closer look at sex education programs, examining the effectiveness of both abstinence-only programs and comprehensive sex education programs in addressing the issue of teen pregnancy.

Abstinence Programs Reduce Teen Pregnancy

Robert Rector, Kirk A. Johnson, and Jennifer A. Marshall

Robert Rector is a domestic policy senior research fellow at the Heritage Foundation, a conservative research and educational institute that investigates domestic, economic, foreign, and defense policy. Kirk A. Johnson is a senior policy analyst at the Heritage Center for Data Analysis, which maintains extensive databases for use by the Heritage Foundation. Jennifer A. Marshall serves as director of domestic policy studies at the Heritage Foundation.

Adolescents who take a virginity pledge have substantially lower levels of sexual activity and better life outcomes when compared with similar adolescents who do not make such a pledge, according to recently released data from the National Longitudinal Study of Adolescent Health (Add Health survey). Specifically, adolescents who make a virginity pledge:

- Are less likely to experience teen pregnancy;

- Are less likely to be sexually active while in high school and as young adults;

- Are less likely to give birth as teens or young adults;

- Are less likely to give birth out of wedlock;

- Are less likely to engage in risky unprotected sex; and

- Will have fewer sexual partners.

In addition, making a virginity pledge is not associated with any long-term negative outcomes. For example, teen pledgers who do become sexually active are not less likely to use contraception.

Robert Rector, Kirk A. Johnson, and Jennifer A. Marshall, "Teens Who Make Virginity Pledges Have Substantially Improved Life Outcomes," Heritage Foundation, September 21, 2004, pp. 1–3, 8, 10, 17. Copyright © 2004 The Heritage Foundation. Reproduced by permission.

Virginity Pledgers Have Less Sex

Data from the National Longitudinal Study of Adolescent Health, which is funded by more than 17 federal agencies, show that the behavior of adolescents who have made a virginity pledge is significantly different from that of peers who have not made a pledge. Teenage girls who have taken a virginity pledge are one-third less likely to experience a pregnancy before age 18. . . .

Teens who make a virginity pledge are far less likely to be sexually active during high school years. Nearly two-thirds of teens who have never taken a pledge are sexually active before age 18; by contrast, only 30 percent of teens who consistently report having made a pledge become sexually active before age 18.

Teens who have made a virginity pledge have almost half as many lifetime sexual partners as non-pledgers have. By the time they reach their early twenties, non-pledgers have had, on average, six different sex partners; pledgers, by contrast, have had three.

Girls who have taken a virginity pledge are one-third less likely to have an out-of-wedlock birth when compared with those who have never taken a pledge. . . .

Girls who make a virginity pledge also have fewer births overall (both marital and nonmarital) as teens and young adults than do girls who do not make pledges. By the time they reach their early twenties, some 27.2 percent of the young women who have never made a virginity pledge have given birth. By contrast, the overall birth rate of peers who have made a pledge is nearly one-third lower, at 19.8 percent.

Because they are less likely to be sexually active, pledging teens are less likely to engage in unprotected sex, especially unprotected nonmarital sex. For example, 28 percent of non-pledging youth reported engaging in unprotected nonmarital sex during the past year, compared with 22 percent of all pledgers and 17 percent of strong pledgers. . . .

Tracked over Time

For more than a decade, organizations such as True Love Waits have encouraged young people to abstain from sexual activity. As part of these programs, young people are encouraged to take a verbal or written pledge to abstain from sex until marriage. In recent years, increased public policy attention has been focused on adolescents who take these "virginity pledges" as policymakers seek to assess the social and behavioral outcomes of such abstinence programs.

One major source of data on teens who have made virginity pledges is the National Longitudinal Study of Adolescent Health, funded by the Department of Health and Human Services and other federal agencies. The Add Health survey started with interviews of junior-high and high-school-aged students in 1994. In that year, and in subsequent interviews, adolescents were asked whether they had ever taken a virginity pledge. The students were tracked through high school and into early adulthood. By 2001, most of the youth in the survey were between the ages of 19 and 25—old enough to evaluate the relationship between pledging as teens and a variety of social outcomes. . . .

Teen Pregnancy Rates Are Lower for Pledgers

The Add Health survey data show that girls who have made a virginity pledge are substantially less likely to experience teen pregnancy (to become pregnant before their 18th birthday) when compared with girls who have not made a pledge. . . . Some 6.5 percent of girls who had made a pledge became pregnant before age 18. The figure for girls who had not made a pledge was about 50 percent higher, at 9.7 percent. Among girls who were strong pledgers [defined as those who consistently reported renewing their pledge over time], the pregnancy rate was lower still: 4.3 percent became pregnant before their 18th birthday—less than half the number among non-pledgers. . . .

Pledgers Are Less Likely to Become Unwed Mothers

Out-of-wedlock childbearing is one of the most important social problems facing our nation. Children born and raised outside marriage are seven times more likely to live in poverty than are children born and raised in intact married families. Children born out of wedlock are five times more likely to be dependent on welfare when compared with those born and raised within wedlock. In addition, children born out of wedlock are more likely to become involved in crime, to have emotional and behavioral problems, to be physically abused, to fail in school, to abuse drugs, and to end up on welfare as adults.

The Add Health survey offers the good news that teenage girls who take a virginity pledge are:

- Substantially less likely to give birth in their teens or early twenties, and

- Less likely to give birth out of wedlock.

Girls who make a virginity pledge are less likely to give birth before their 18th birthday. Some 1.8 percent of the strong pledgers surveyed had given birth before 18; the rate for non-pledging girls was twice as high, at 3.8 percent.

Pledgers are significantly less likely than non-pledgers to engage in unprotected sexual activity.

By the time they reach their early twenties, non-pledging young women remain far more likely to have become pregnant and to have given birth than are peers who have made a pledge. . . . By the time of the [third follow-up survey in 2001] some 27.2 percent of non-pledging girls had given birth to at least one child. By contrast, about one-third fewer (19.8 percent) of the girls who "had ever made a pledge" had given birth.

The contrast in out-of-wedlock childbearing is even stronger. By [the time] of the survey in 2001, 20.6 percent of non-pledging girls had given birth out of wedlock. The rate of out-of-wedlock births among strong pledgers was nearly 50 percent lower, at 10.8 percent.

Out-of-wedlock childbearing has major long-term negative effects on mothers and children. Although some pledgers did experience this problem, as a whole, teens who made pledges were much more likely to avoid this pitfall. Moreover, the lower rate of out-of-wedlock childbirth among pledgers was not the result of "shotgun marriages" (marriages that occur after an accidental pregnancy). Teen pledgers were no more likely to have shotgun marriages than were non-pledgers.

Finally, pledgers had fewer abortions than did non-pledgers. The abortion rates were 7.8 percent for non-pledgers, 5.7 percent for all pledgers, and 4.2 percent for strong pledgers. However, given the low rates reported, these differences are not statistically significant. . . .

Pledgers Have Lower Rates of Unprotected Sexual Activity

Pledgers are significantly less likely than non-pledgers to engage in unprotected sexual activity (i.e., to have intercourse without contraception). While previous reports have suggested that sexually active pledgers are less likely to use contraception than non-pledgers are, examination of the . . . data [from the third follow-up] of the Add Health survey does not confirm this. In fact, pledgers who are sexually active are slightly more likely to use contraception than are their counterparts among the non-pledging group. However, the difference between the groups is not statistically significant.

Moreover, examination of sexually active youths presents only part of the picture. As noted previously, pledgers are far more likely to abstain from sexual activity entirely. Thus, when all youths (both those who are sexually active and those who are inactive) are examined, the data show that pledgers are substantially less likely to endanger themselves or others through unprotected sexual activity. . . . [The data show that] 17.1 percent of strong pledgers reported having engaged in unprotected sex in the last survey year, compared to 28.2 percent of non-pledgers. . . . Pledging is linked to a significant reduction in risky behavior. . . .

Abstinence-Only Education Is Effective

Teens who make virginity pledges promise to remain virgins until marriage. While many pledgers fail to meet that goal, as a group, teens who make virginity pledges have substantially improved behaviors compared with non-pledgers. Teens who make pledges have better life outcomes and are far less likely to engage in risky behaviors. As a whole, teen pledgers will have fewer sexual partners and are less likely to become sexually active in high school. Pledgers are less likely to experience teen pregnancy, less likely to give birth out of wedlock, and less likely to engage in unprotected sexual activity. These positive outcomes are linked to the act of making the pledge itself and are not the result of social background factors.

Parents continue to support abstinence values and to realize that good abstinence education programs can positively affect youth behavior.

In addition, there are no negative risky behaviors associated with taking a virginity pledge. For example, pledgers who become sexually active are not less likely to use contraception. Thus, teens have everything to gain and nothing to lose from virginity pledge programs. Such programs appear to have a strong and significant effect in encouraging positive and constructive behavior among youth.

Today's teens, however, live in a sex-saturated culture, and positive influences that counteract the tide of permissiveness are scattered and weak. Relatively few youth are exposed to the affirmative messages coming from virginity pledge programs and similar abstinence education programs. Sadly, despite polls showing that nearly all parents want youth to be taught a strong abstinence message, abstinence education is rare in American schools. While it is true that, bowing to popular pressure, most current sex education curricula claim that they promote abstinence, in reality, these programs pay little more than lip service to the topic. Most, in fact, are permeated by anti-abstinence themes.

Still, parents continue to support abstinence values and to realize that good abstinence education programs can positively affect youth behavior. It is regrettable that most schools fail to meet either parents' expectations or students' needs.

School-Based Sex Education Programs Effectively Address Teen Pregnancy

Joycelyn Elders, interviewed by Priscilla Pardini

Joycelyn Elders is the former surgeon general of the United States. She was forced to resign in December 1994 after commenting that children should be taught about masturbation in schools. Elders is on the staff at Children's Hospital in Little Rock, Arkansas, and on the faculty at the School of Medicine at the University of Arkansas. She is also working on a book, The Dreaded M Word. *Elders was interviewed by Priscilla Pardini, a freelance writer, for* Rethinking Schools, *a periodical that discusses education issues.*

Priscilla Pardini: What's wrong with abstinence-only sexuality education programs?

Joycelyn Elders: Nothing, in the very early grades. If we did a really good job in the first 10 or 12 years of children's lives teaching them about abstinence, as well as about honesty and integrity and responsibility and how to make good decisions, we would not have to be talking to them at 15 about not getting engaged in sex.

But we haven't done that. Mothers have been teaching abstinence, schools have been teaching abstinence, preachers have been preaching abstinence for years. Yet more than three million teens get STDs [sexually transmitted diseases] every year, and we still have the highest teen pregnancy, abortion, and birth rates in the industrialized world. But we seem to feel that we don't need to educate our children about their sexuality. That makes absolutely no sense. We all know the vows of abstinence break far more easily than latex condoms.

Joycelyn Elders, interviewed by Priscilla Pardini, "Vows of Abstinence Break More Easily than Latex Condoms: An Interview with Joycelyn Elders," *Rethinking Schools*, vol. 12, Summer 1998. © 1998 Rethinking Schools. Reproduced by permission.

Teens need a comprehensive sexuality program that gives them all the information they need to become empowered and responsible for preventing pregnancy and disease. We have to stop trying to legislate morals and instead teach responsibility. Abstinence-only does not do that. You can't be responsible if you don't have the information.

But is school the best place for sexuality education? Isn't this better left to parents?

I have no problem leaving it to parents, if you have parents who can and will do it. But we have many dysfunctional parents—some on drugs, some into alcohol, some who are stressed out, and some who just don't know how to talk to their children about sex. Then the responsibility belongs to the community. And since the only place we've got access to every child is in school, we need to use our schools to teach about sexuality. We don't depend on parents to teach math and English and science and geography. So why should we depend on parents to teach children all of their social and behavioral skills?

Teachers say they don't have enough time as it is to adequately cover academic subjects. Doesn't sexuality education cut into precious time now allotted to basics such as reading and math?

I think teachers are doing a wonderful job—the best they can under difficult circumstances. But what good is knowing math and science if you don't know how to protect yourself? The fact is, we invest more money in prisons than we do in schools. We're putting out a dragnet when we ought to be putting out a safety net.

Our children, from the time they enter kindergarten through 12th grade, spend 18,000 hours watching TV, but only 12,000 hours in reading and math classes and only 46 hours in health education classes. I say let's take away some of the TV time—and devote more hours to the school day, to summer school.

How early should sexuality education start? What kinds of topics should be covered in the early years?

As early as kindergarten children need to be taught to respect their bodies, to eat in healthy ways and to feel good about themselves. They need to know how to make good decisions and how to deal with conflict in non-violent ways. People who feel good about themselves feel in control of their lives and can make decisions that are right for them. Years later, these children, if they choose to be sexually active, will probably also choose to use a latex condom to protect themselves. But if you're not in control of your sexuality, you can't control your life. Those are the people who end up saying, "It just happened."

How can teachers evaluate whether material is age-appropriate for their students? Can you offer some guidelines for elementary, middle and high school?

There are a lot of high-quality, well-tested curricula out there that are age-appropriate. Even very young kids should know that anytime anyone touches you in a way you don't want to be touched, even if it is your parents, you have to tell somebody. That message needs to start in kindergarten, but also needs to be repeated and reinforced. Older kids should learn about the menstrual cycle, that if they choose to be sexually active they can get diseases or get pregnant. They should know that you can get pregnant the first time you have sex . . . that you can get pregnant if you have sex standing up.

By high school, you need to be teaching them more about responsibility and equality—that boys and girls have equal responsibility for their sexuality. They should be taught about date rape, about birth control. They should be taught to assume that anytime they have sex they are risking—boys and girls—AIDS, sexually transmitted disease, and becoming a parent. At this point, when you simply tell them they should "just say no," they look out the window and start singing. It's too little too late.

What about the charge that teaching teens about sexuality actually increases sexual activity?

There has never, never been any study that has documented that teaching young people about sex increases sexual activity, and most studies say it decreases sexual activity. In fact, according to [one] study ["Impact of High School Condom Availability Program on Sexual Attitudes and Behaviors," *Family Planning Perspectives*, March/April, 1998] even when condoms were made available in a high school, sexual activity did not increase.

How serious are teen pregnancy, STDs and HIV among teens?

There are more than 3 million STDs a year reported in those under 19 years of age. Genital herpes—which cannot be cured—has increased almost 30% in young people in the last eight or nine years. The pregnancy rate is slightly down, but there are still almost 900,000 teen pregnancies a year. When it comes to HIV, the largest increase in cases is seen in teenagers. This is serious. The stakes are very high.

Yet, sex education has been part of the curriculum in many schools for many years. Why isn't it working?

We've not had comprehensive K-12 sexuality education. We're still out there giving kids an annual AIDS lecture. We might as well keep that. We don't teach math by giving one lecture a year. You have to do it all the time and keep reinforcing it. We're not making a committed effort to change things. What we're doing is criticizing and blaming. The problem is, we're willing to sacrifice our children to preserve our Victorian attitudes. We know what to do. We know how to do it. We just don't have the will to get it done.

In the 1960s, when we found out our children were behind in math and science, we added courses in math and science. So if we want to address the social problems our children are having now, we have to put in the programs to do it.

How should a school administrator respond if a parent or group of parents demands that an abstinence-only curriculum be taught?

A superintendent should agree with the parents and put in an abstinence-only program for kindergarten and elementary students. When it comes to older students, he really needs to tell other parents what's going on so they can rise up and fight. Ultimately, a superintendent has to do what his board members tell him to do. But it's the parents who carry the big stick. Parents can get anything they want, and two major studies have shown that most parents want comprehensive sexuality education, with condom availability, in the schools. Yet, because of their silence, they let this other side get their way and destroy their children.

What is the relationship between public health departments, public schools, and the U.S. Surgeon General's office?

There should be a marriage between schools and public health. We should have health education programs in schools along with school-based clinics that would be easily accessible to students and affordable. Now, many young people don't know where to go or don't have the money to pay for health services. We also need to teach people how to be healthy. We have a health-illiterate society, and one place to correct that is in the schools. I think the Surgeon General has a role to play in promoting good health practices and focusing on prevention—to try and make this country as healthy as it can be.

Several Pregnancy Prevention Programs Deliver Strong Results

Catherine Gewertz

Catherine Gewertz is an assistant editor for Education Week, *a publication of the nonprofit Editorial Projects in Education, Inc. This Washington, D.C.–based organization works to help teaching professionals understand various issues facing American education.*

A fter years of elusive answers to the problem of teenage pregnancy, a leading group involved in the issue has released a new and more optimistic report [in 2001] that outlines several effective and varied tactics in deterring adolescent sex and pregnancy.

The review of existing research, conducted by the National Campaign to Prevent Teen Pregnancy, identifies eight programs that the report says have delivered strong results.

Several Programs Are Working

Douglas Kirby, who performed the review for the Washington-based campaign, said his look at other studies was encouraging, especially in the wake of a report he wrote in 1997, "No Easy Answers." That report found little documented success among programs to prevent teenage pregnancy.

"We now have not one, but multiple ways of reducing teen pregnancy," Mr. Kirby said in an interview just after the new report, "Emerging Answers," was released [in 2001]. . . . "We have strong evidence of multiple programs that do work, and we now know what those are. That gives communities a number of options."

Catherine Gewertz, "Clear, Consistent Messages Help Deter Teen Pregnancy, Study Finds," *Education Week*, vol. 20, no. 39, June 6, 2001, p. 5. Reproduced by permission.

Mr. Kirby is a senior research scientist at ETR Associates in Scotts Valley, Calif., a nonprofit training and research group that developed and markets two of the five programs for sex and HIV education cited in the report as being successful. He also serves on the board of the National Campaign to Prevent Teen Pregnancy, a ... nonpartisan, nonprofit group financed largely by private donations.

Clear Messages Are Vital

The review found that some sex and HIV education programs that include discussion of contraceptives can delay the onset of sexual activity by teenagers and reduce its frequency. It indicates that those programs do not, as some critics have contended, increase sexual activity.

One of the key qualities that make sex education programs effective, the report concludes, is the delivery and reinforcement of a clear and consistent message about abstaining from sex or using contraception. It is also important that such programs last more than a few hours, address the social pressures that influence teenage sexual behavior, and provide basic, accurate information about the risks of sexual activity, the report says.

Abstinence-Only Programs Still Under Debate

No conclusions can be drawn about the effectiveness of abstinence-only programs, according to the review. Such instruction has become increasingly popular since the 1996 welfare-reform law has made more than $80 million in state and federal aid available annually for such programs.

But Mr. Kirby said that there has been too little solid research done on abstinence-only programs to gauge their effectiveness. One report [in 2001], for instance, found that 16- and 17-year-olds who had made "virginity pledges" tended to delay sexual activity longer than those who hadn't, but that the pledges had made no difference for 18-year-olds.

Bridget Maher, a policy analyst with the Washington-based Family Research Council, which advocates abstinence-only approaches, offered a different perspective on the sex education research.

"We know that teaching kids to be sexually abstinent until marriage is the only sure way that they won't become pregnant," she said.

Service-Learning Programs Are Effective

The national campaign's report says that programs can be effective in preventing pregnancy and delaying teenage sexual activity even if they do not focus on sex. The review found, for instance, that girls who had participated in service-learning programs were less likely to become pregnant.

The report singles out for particular praise a long-term, comprehensive program created by Michael Carrera of the Children's Aid Society in New York City. That project offers sex education to teenagers, but also includes tutoring and homework help, aid with college applications, sports and art activities, job assistance, and comprehensive health care.

An examination of the results from 12 sites that use the program showed that female participants reduced their pregnancy rates by half and delayed engaging in sex during the three years they were in the program. It did not, however, affect the behavior of its male participants.

The study comes at [a] time when teenage pregnancy rates have been declining for a decade. But it notes that more than four in 10 teenage girls still get pregnant before they turn 20, resulting in 900,000 such pregnancies a year.

Abstinence-Only Programs Do Not Reduce Teen Pregnancy

Cory Richards

Since 1975 Cory Richards has been with the Alan Guttmacher Institute, a nonprofit organization that focuses on sexual and re-productive health issues, policy analysis, and public education. Richards writes extensively about sexual and reproductive health policy issues and edits the institute's quarterly policy review.

Helping young people to understand the benefits of delay-ing sexual activity and to resist peer pressure is, and clearly should be, a cornerstone of sex education in the United States. Virtually no one disputes the importance of abstinence education. But support for abstinence-only education which ignores or actually denigrates the effectiveness of contracep-tives and condoms is not based on scientific evidence; rather it is driven by a subjective moral and, for many, religious agenda. The nation's leading medical, public-health and edu-cational organizations endorse sex education that includes positive messages about the value of delaying sexual activity along with information about condoms and contraceptive use to avoid sexually transmitted diseases [STDs] and unintended pregnancy. Public-opinion polls show that this also is the po-sition of parents, teachers and young people themselves in the United States.

What Does the Evidence Show?

- Teenagers and young adults are at risk of unintended pregnancies and STDs for almost a decade between the time they initiate sexual activity and when they get married. By their 18th birthday, six in 10 teenage women and nearly seven in 10 teenage men have had sexual intercourse.

- Teenage pregnancy happens. Nearly 900,000 American teenagers (ages 15–19) become pregnant each year, and almost four in five (78 percent) of these pregnancies are unintended.

- Other countries do better. Despite recent declines, the United States has one of the highest teenage pregnancy rates in the developed world. U.S. teenagers are twice as likely to become pregnant as teenagers in England, Wales or Canada and nine times as likely as those in the Netherlands and Japan.

- Teenagers and young adults are at risk of STDs and HIV/AIDS. Four million teenagers acquire an STD annually. Half of the 40,000 new cases of HIV infection in the United States each year occur to individuals younger than age 25. This means that every hour of every day an average of two young people become infected with HIV.

- Contraceptives and condoms are effective. While it is true that successfully abstaining from sexual activity is the only 100 percent guaranteed way of preventing pregnancy and disease, abstinence can and does fail. Extensive research demonstrates that correct and consistent use of contraceptives, including condoms, radically reduces one's risk of pregnancy and disease among those who are sexually active.

Despite the clear need to help young people make safe decisions regarding sexual activity so that they can delay the initiation of sexual intercourse and protect themselves from unintended pregnancy and STDs when they become sexually active, U.S. policymakers continue to promote school-based, abstinence-until-marriage education that fails to provide accurate and complete information about condoms or other contraceptives.

Abstinence-Only Education Fails Youth

Overall, federal and matching funding from states for abstinence education that excludes information about contraception has totaled more than $700 million since 1996. There is, on the other hand, no federal program dedicated to supporting comprehensive sex education. Federal law contains an extremely narrow eight-point definition of abstinence-only education that sets forth specific messages to be taught, including that sex outside of marriage for people of any age is likely to have harmful physical and psychological effects. Because funded programs must promote abstinence exclusively, they are prohibited from advocating contraceptive use. They thus have a choice: They either must refrain from discussing contraceptive methods altogether or limit their discussion to contraceptive failure rates. Further, in many cases federal law prevents these programs from using their private funds to provide young people with information about contraception or safer-sex practices. Yet even today, many policymakers remain unfamiliar with this extremely restrictive brand of abstinence-only education required by federal law.

Despite similar levels of sexual activity among American teenagers and their [foreign] counterparts ... teenagers in this country fare worse in terms of pregnancy and STDs.

Considerable scientific evidence shows that certain programs that include information about both abstinence and contraception help teenagers delay the onset of sexual activity, reduce their number of sexual partners and increase contraceptive use when they do become sexually active. Indeed, leading medical, public-health and educational organizations, including the American Medical Association, the American Academy of Pediatrics, the American College of Obstetricians and Gynecologists and the National Institutes of Health, support sex-education programs that both stress abstinence and teach young people about the importance of protecting themselves against unintended pregnancy and disease when they become sexually active.

In contrast, there have been few rigorous evaluations of programs focusing exclusively on abstinence. None of these has found evidence that these programs either delay sexual activity or reduce teen pregnancy. Finally, research on virginity-pledge programs and HIV-prevention efforts suggests that education and strategies that promote abstinence but withhold information about contraceptives [and condoms, in particular] may have harmful health consequences by deterring the use of contraceptives when teens become sexually active.

Four in 10 teachers either do not teach about contraceptive methods . . . or teach that they are ineffective in preventing pregnancy and STDs.

Despite similar levels of sexual activity among American teenagers and their counterparts in other developed countries, teenagers in this country fare worse in terms of pregnancy and STDs. U.S. teenagers are less likely to use contraceptives, particularly the pill or other highly effective hormonal methods. U.S. teenagers also have shorter relationships and thus more sexual partners over time, increasing their risk for STDs. Evidence from other developed countries, moreover, suggests that when teenagers are provided with comprehensive education about pregnancy and STD prevention in schools and community settings, levels of teenage pregnancy, childbearing and STDs are low. Adults in these other countries give clear and unambiguous messages that sex should occur within committed relationships and that sexually active teenagers are expected to take steps to protect themselves and their partners from pregnancy and STDs.

Students' Needs Are Often Unmet

On certain topics, there is a large gap between what sex-education teachers believe they should cover and what they actually are teaching. The great majority of sex-education teachers think that instruction should cover factual information about birth control and abortion, the correct way to use a condom and sexual orientation. However, far fewer actually teach these topics, either because they are prohibited from doing so or because they fear such teaching would create controversy. As a result, a startling one in four teachers believes they are not meeting their students' needs for information.

The gap between what sex-education teachers think should be covered and what they actually teach particularly is acute when it comes to contraception. Sex-education teachers almost universally believe that students should be provided with basic factual information about birth control, but one in four teachers are prohibited by school policies from doing so. Overall, four in 10 teachers either do not teach about contraceptive methods [including condoms] or teach that they are ineffective in preventing pregnancy and STDs.

What many students are being taught in sex-education classes does not reflect public opinion about what they should be learning. Americans overwhelmingly support sex education that includes information about both abstinence and contraception. Moreover, public-opinion polls consistently show that parents of middle-school and high-school students support this kind of sex education over classes that teach only abstinence.

Parents also want sex-education classes to cover topics that are perceived as controversial by many school administrators and teachers. At least three-quarters of parents say that sex-education classes should cover how to use condoms and other forms of birth control, as well as provide information on abortion and sexual orientation. Yet these topics are the very ones that teachers often do not cover. Finally, two out of three parents say that significantly more classroom time should be devoted to sex education.

Abstinence-only programs . . . can undermine students' confidence in contraception by providing unbalanced evidence of its ineffectiveness.

Similarly, students report that they want more information about sexual- and reproductive-health issues than they are receiving in school. Nearly one-half of junior-high and high-school students report wanting more factual information about birth control and HIV/AIDS and other STDs, as well as what to do in the event of rape or sexual assault, how to talk with a partner about birth control and how to handle pressure to have sex. Young people also need to receive information sooner: More than one-quarter of students become sexually active before they receive even a rudimentary level of sex education such as "how to say no to sex."

Protecting Kids Requires a Balanced Approach

Abstinence-only programs also can undermine students' confidence in contraception by providing unbalanced evidence of its ineffectiveness. These programs miss the opportunity to provide students with the skills they need to use contraceptives more, and more effectively. Instead students may leave the program thinking that pregnancy and STDs are inevitable once they begin having sex.

To be sure, promoting abstinence to young, unmarried people as a valid and realistic lifestyle choice should remain a key component of sex education. But those who argue that this is the only message that should be provided to young people are misguided. The evidence strongly suggests that sex in the teenage years and certainly prior to marriage, which now typically occurs in the mid-20s, is and will continue to be common, both in this country and around the world. Undermining people's confidence in the effectiveness of condoms and other contraceptive methods as a means of scaring them out of having sex is just plain wrong. Protecting our young people requires a balanced approach that emphasizes all the key means of prevention including effective contraceptive and condom use, as well as delaying sex. Ultimately, only such a comprehensive approach will provide young people with the tools they need to protect themselves and to become sexually healthy adults.

Most Abstinence-Only Programs Contain Inaccurate Information

Minority Staff Special Investigations Division of the U.S. House of Representatives Committee on Government Reform

The House Special Investigations Division was formed in 1998 by Representative Henry A. Waxman to study issues important to the minority members of the Committee on Government Reform, as well as other members of Congress. The Committee on Government Reform has the jurisdiction to investigate any matter with federal policy implications.

Under the [George W.] Bush Administration, there has been a dramatic increase in federal support for "abstinence-only" education programs. Also called "abstinence education" or "abstinence-until-marriage education," these programs promote abstinence from all sexual activity, usually until marriage, as the only way to reduce the risks of pregnancy, disease, and other potential consequences of sex. The programs define sexual activity broadly and do not teach basic facts about contraception.

In fiscal year 2001, under the last budget passed under the [Bill] Clinton Administration, abstinence-only education programs received approximately $80 million in federal funding. Since then, federal abstinence-only funding has more than doubled, with the final omnibus appropriations bill containing $167 million in funding for fiscal year 2005. President Bush had proposed $270 million for abstinence-only programs in fiscal year 2005. . . .

Minority Staff Special Investigations Division of the U.S. House of Representatives Committee on Government Reform, "The Content of Federally Funded Abstinence-Only Education Programs," a report prepared for Rep. Henry A. Waxman, December 2004.

Accuracy Is an Issue

There have been several studies of the effectiveness of abstinence-only education. These studies have found that abstinence-only education does not appear to decrease teen pregnancy or the risk of sexually transmitted diseases [STDs]. In the most comprehensive analysis of teen pregnancy prevention programs, researchers found that "the few rigorous studies of abstinence-only curricula that have been completed to date do not show any overall effect on sexual behavior or contraceptive use."

One recent study of abstinence-only programs found that they may actually increase participants' risk. Columbia University researchers found that while virginity "pledge" programs helped some participants to delay sex, 88% still had premarital sex, and their rates of sexually transmitted diseases showed no statistically significant difference from those of nonpledgers. Virginity pledgers were also less likely to use contraception when they did have sex and were less likely to seek STD testing despite comparable infection rates.

In contrast, comprehensive sex education that both encourages abstinence and teaches about effective contraceptive use has been shown in many studies to delay sex, reduce the frequency of sex, and increase the use of condoms and other contraceptives.

While there have been evaluations of the effectiveness of abstinence-only education programs, the content of the curricula taught in these programs has received little attention. The federal government does not review or approve the accuracy of the information presented in abstinence-only programs. . . .

At the request of Rep. Henry Waxman [D-CA], this report is a comprehensive evaluation of the content of the curricula used in federally funded abstinence-only education programs. It is based on a review of the most popular abstinence-only curricula used by grantees in the SPRANS [Special Programs of Regional and National Significance Community-Based Abstinence Education] program.

Multiple [abstinence-only] curricula provide false information about condoms and HIV transmission.

To conduct this evaluation, the Special Investigations Division obtained from the Health Resources and Services Administration the program summaries of the 100 organizations that received SPRANS abstinence funding during fiscal year 2003. Each summary contains a proposal listing the curricula that the program intends to use. The Special Investigations Division then acquired each curriculum that was listed by at least five funding recipients. Thirteen curricula met this criterion.

The 13 curricula were reviewed for scientific accuracy. For several curricula with a separate teacher's guide, both the student and teacher manuals were included. The review was intended to provide an overall assessment of the accuracy of the curricula, not to identify all potential errors. . . .

Condoms Under Fire

According to the Centers for Disease Control and Prevention (CDC), "Latex condoms, when used consistently and correctly, are highly effective in preventing the transmission of HIV, the virus that causes AIDS." Contrary to this scientific consensus, multiple [abstinence-only] curricula provide false information about condoms and HIV transmission.

Several curricula cite an erroneous 1993 study of condom effectiveness that has been discredited by federal health officials. The 1993 study, by Dr. Susan Weller, looked at a variety of condom effectiveness studies and concluded that condoms reduce HIV transmission by 69%. Dr. Weller's conclusions were rejected by the Department of Health and Human Services, which issued a statement in 1997 informing the public that "FDA [Food and Drug Administration] and CDC believe this analysis was flawed." The Department cited numerous methodological problems, including the mixing of data on consistent condom use with data on inconsistent condom use, and found that Dr. Weller's calculation of a 69% effectiveness rate was based on "serious error." In fact, CDC noted that "[o]ther studies of discordant couples—more recent and larger than the ones Weller reviewed, and conducted over several years—have demonstrated that consistent condom use is highly effective at preventing HIV infection."

Despite these findings, several [SPRANS-approved] curricula refer approvingly to the Weller study. One curriculum teaches: "A meticulous review of condom effectiveness was reported by Dr. Susan Weller in 1993. She found that condoms were even less likely to protect people from HIV infection. Condoms appear to reduce the risk of heterosexual HIV infection by only 69%." Another curriculum that cites Dr. Weller's data claims: "In heterosexual sex, condoms fail to prevent HIV approximately 31% of the time."

Other abstinence-only curricula contest CDC's finding that "latex condoms provide an essentially impermeable barrier to particles the size of STD pathogens." These curricula rely on the false idea that HIV and other pathogens can "pass through" condoms. One curriculum instructs students to:

> Think on a microscopic level. Sperm cells, STI [sexually transmitted infections] organisms, and HIV cannot be seen with the naked eye—you need a microscope. Any imperfections in the contraceptive not visible to the eye, could allow sperm, STI, or HIV to pass through. . . . The size difference between a sperm cell and the HIV virus can be roughly related to the difference between the size of a football field and a football.

The same curriculum states, "The actual ability of condoms to prevent the transmission of HIV/AIDS even if the product is intact, is not definitively known." This distorts CDC's finding and scientific consensus. . . .

Several curricula distort public health data on the effectiveness of condoms in preventing other sexually transmitted diseases. One curriculum claims: "If condoms were effective against STDs, it would be reasonable to expect that an increase in condom usage would correlate to a decrease in STDs overall—which is not the case. Rather, as condom usage has increased, so have rates of STDs." Another states: "[T]he popular claim that 'condoms help prevent the spread of STDs,' is not supported by the data."

These assertions are wrong. The curricula fail to note that rates of important sexually transmitted diseases, such as syphilis and gonorrhea, have been dropping over the past decade. Contrary to the assertions in the curricula, the most recent data show that consistent condom use is associated with:

- Reduced acquisition of syphilis by women and by men;

- Reduced acquisition of gonorrhea by women;

- Reduced acquisition of urethral infection by men; and

- Faster regression of HPV [human papilloma virus]-related lesions on the cervix and penis, and faster clearance of genital HPV infection in women. . . .

Failure Rates Are Exaggerated

None of the curricula provides information on how to select a birth control method and use it effectively. However, several curricula exaggerate condom failure rates in preventing pregnancy.

Failure rates for contraception are calculated as the probability of a couple experiencing pregnancy when relying primarily on the contraceptive method over the course of one year. "Typical use" failure rates are often higher than "perfect use" rates largely because the former include people who use the method incorrectly or only sometimes. Condoms have a typical use contraceptive failure rate of approximately 15% and a perfect use failure rate of 2% to 3%.

According to the World Health Organization, the difference between typical and perfect use "is due primarily to inconsistent and incorrect use, not to condom failure. Condom failure—the device breaking or slipping off during intercourse—is uncommon."

Several curricula misrepresent the data to exaggerate how often condoms fail to prevent pregnancy:

- The parent guide for one curriculum understates condom effectiveness by falsely describing "actual use" as "scrupulous." It states: "When used by real people in real-life situations, research confirms that 14 percent of the women who use condoms scrupulously for birth control become pregnant within a year." In fact, for couples who use condoms "scrupulously," the 2% to 3% failure rate applies.

- Two other curricula understate condom effectiveness by neglecting to explain that failure rates represent the chance of pregnancy over the course of a year. One states: "Couples who use condoms to avoid a pregnancy have a failure rate of 15%." The other claims: "The typical failure rate for the male condom is 14% in preventing pregnancy." These statements inaccurately suggest that the chance of pregnancy is 14% to 15% after each act of protected intercourse. In addition, they do not make clear that most condom "failure" is due to incorrect or inconsistent use.

Another curriculum presents misleading information about the risk of pregnancy from sexual activity other than intercourse. The curriculum erroneously states that touching another person's genitals "can result in pregnancy." In fact, the source cited for this contention specifically states that "remaining a virgin all but eliminates the possibility of becoming pregnant."

Risks of Abortion Overstated

A high number of the programs receiving SPRANS funding are formally opposed to abortion access. Multiple SPRANS recipients are explicitly pro-life organizations such as "crisis pregnancy centers." Several of the curricula used by these and other recipients give misleading information about the physical and psychological effects of legal abortions.

By their nature, abstinence-only curricula teach moral judgments alongside scientific facts.

For example, one curriculum relies on numerous outdated sources to present a distorted and exaggerated view of the dangers of legal abortion. Much of the data cited is from the 1970s, yet according to the American Medical Association Council on Scientific Affairs, "[t]he risk of major complications from abortion-related procedures declined dramatically between 1970 and 1990." The curriculum inaccurately describes the risks of sterility, premature birth and mental retardation, and ectopic pregnancies:

- The curriculum states, "Sterility: Studies show that five to ten percent of women will never again be pregnant after having a legal abortion." In fact, obstetrics textbooks teach that "[f]ertility is not altered by an elective abortion."

- The curriculum states, "Premature birth, a major cause of mental retardation, is increased following the abortion of the first pregnancy." In fact, obstetrics textbooks teach that vacuum aspiration, the method used in most abortions in the United States, "results in no increased incidence of midtrimester spontaneous abortions, preterm delivery, or low-birthweight infants in subsequent pregnancies." . . .

Curricula Blur Religion and Science

By their nature, abstinence-only curricula teach moral judgments alongside scientific facts. The SPRANS program mandates, for example, that programs teach that having sex only within marriage "is the expected standard of human sexual activity." In some of the curricula, the moral judgments are explicitly religious. For example, in a newsletter accompanying one popular curriculum, the author laments that as a result of societal change, "No longer were we valued as spiritual beings made by a loving Creator." The curriculum's author closes the section by signing, "In His Service."

In other curricula, moral judgments are misleadingly offered as scientific fact.

Although religions and moral codes offer different answers to the question of when life begins, some abstinence-only curricula present specific religious views on this question as scientific fact. One curriculum teaches: "Conception, also known as fertilization, occurs when one sperm unites with one egg in the upper third of the fallopian tube. This is when life begins." Another states: "Fertilization (or conception) occurs when one of the father's sperm unites with the mother's ovum (egg). At this instant a new human life is formed."

Over two-thirds of abstinence-only education programs . . . are using curricula with multiple scientific and medical inaccuracies.

A related question, also answered differently by people of differing beliefs, is whether a developing fetus is a person. Several curricula offer as scientific fact moral or religious definitions of early fetuses as babies or people, in the process supplying inaccurate descriptions of their developmental state.

One curriculum that describes fetuses as "babies" describes the blastocyst, technically a ball of 107 to 256 cells at the beginning of uterine implantation, as "snuggling" into the uterus:

After conception, the tiny baby moves down the fallopian tube toward the mother's uterus. About the sixth to tenth day after conception, when the baby is no bigger than this dot (.), baby snuggles into the soft nest in the lining of the mother's uterus. . . .

Scientific Errors Common

In addition to the inaccurate and misleading information discussed above, a number of the abstinence-only curricula contain erroneous information about basic scientific facts. These errors cover a variety of issues:

- *Human Genetics.* One curriculum states: "Twenty-four chromosomes from the mother and twenty-four chromosomes from the father join to create this new individual." In fact, human cells have 23 chromosomes from each parent, for a total of 46 in each body cell. The same curriculum also teaches: "Girls produce only female ovum, boys, however, have both male and female sperm." This too is inaccurate. Females produce ova with X chromosomes, and males produce sperm with either X or Y chromosomes. These combine to make an XX combination (female) or an XY combination (male).

- *Infectious Disease.* One curriculum defines "sexually transmitted infections" as "bacterial infections that are acute and usually can be cured" and defines "sexually transmitted diseases" as "infections that are viral in nature, chronic, and usually can not be cured, but rather controlled through treatment." In fact, these terms are used interchangeably in medicine, and the program's definitions are not widely accepted. . . .

Under the Bush Administration, federal support for abstinence-only education has risen dramatically. This report finds that over two-thirds of abstinence-only education programs funded by the largest federal abstinence initiative are using curricula with multiple scientific and medical inaccuracies. These curricula contain misinformation about condoms, abortion, and basic scientific facts.

School-Based Sex Education Programs Ineffectively Address Teen Pregnancy

Marjorie Coeyman

Marjorie Coeyman is a staff writer for the Christian Science Monitor.

In some classrooms, sex education means a dark message about the frightening potential consequences of sex outside marriage. Yet in others, a class of the same title involves graphic, practical information about contraceptives, presented with the casual expectation that these are things every teen needs to know.

Sex Ed Is a Touchy Subject

There are few topics in US public education that ignite more emotion—or bridge more divergent viewpoints—than sex ed. In an age when Americans talk about sex more freely than ever, they still struggle with the question of what to tell their children.

When it comes to deciding what should be taught about the subject in school, it is hard to find an inch of common ground in what has become a highly polarized battleground.

"[Sex education] has become an ideological war, full of very fuzzy thinking," says Douglas Besharov, the Jacobs Scholar at the American Enterprise Institute [a conservative think tank] in Washington. "I blame this whole thing on the adults—on the left and the right—who have confused this mightily."

On the one side of the divide are proponents of "abstinence-only" programs. These programs teach that sex

Marjorie Coeyman, "Schools Stumble Over Sex Education," *Christian Science Monitor*, July 22, 2003, p. 13. Copyright © 2003 The Christian Science Publishing Society. All rights reserved. Reproduced by permission from *Christian Science Monitor* (www.csmonitor.com).

outside of marriage, at any age, is wrong. Because advocates of this approach are concerned about presenting a mixed message, most insist that these classes may not include any information about contraceptives.

On the other side are those who favor what is called "comprehensive" sex education. This approach may include teaching students that abstinence outside marriage is either one option or perhaps even the best course, but this message is followed up with practical information about sex. Generally this focuses on how contraceptives work, where to get them, and why they are important.

The two sides find themselves almost entirely at odds.

Most Programs Fail Our Teens

Abstinence-only supporters protest that comprehensive sex ed confuses teens by encouraging promiscuity. But those who favor comprehensive sex ed worry that failing to give kids basic information about sex—and particularly about contraceptives—only increases the danger of sexually transmitted diseases and teenage pregnancies.

However, somewhere in between these two sets of concerns, some argue, lies a broad middle ground in which students are being deprived of something more essential: enough context in which to understand the information they're being given

It's hard sometimes to be patient with either side of this debate, Mr. Besharov says. The abstinence-only supporters are so adamant about preventing sex outside marriage that they may squelch useful information. But at the same time, he says, those who favor comprehensive sex ed often fail to distinguish between the needs of a 12-year-old and those of a 17-year-old.

They fail to appreciate that, "beyond some kind of moral issue, having sex too early can be horribly damaging to young people," he says.

Shifting Priorities and Ideologies Share Curriculum

When sex ed was first introduced into US public schools in the 1940s, it was not done with concern for the morals or emotions of teenagers but rather to control sexually transmitted diseases and cut back on teen pregnancies. But in recent years conservative politicians have embraced abstinence programs as the most effective approach to questions of teen sex.

Abstinence programs received some government support as early as the 1980s, but in 1996 the Welfare Reform Act—signed into law by President [Bill] Clinton—upped the ante by providing $50 million annually for their propagation. But it's been under the [George W.] Bush administration that they have grown far more rapidly.

The federal government now funds such programs at $120 million annually, with a proposal on the table to increase that.... States that accept such funding must agree that sex ed classes will make it their "exclusive purpose" to teach "the social, psychological, and health gains to be realized by abstaining from sexual activity."

Today, 95 percent of US public secondary schools teach some kind of sex ed. Comprehensive sex ed is still the favored approach. But with increasing funds becoming available for them, abstinence-only programs are expected to grow rapidly over the next few years—a development that worries those who want a broader approach.

Few High Quality Programs Exist

"Delay [sexual] activity, decrease the number of partners, and increase use of contraceptives," says Tamara Kreinin, president and CEO of the Sexuality Information and Education Council of the US. Those, she says, should be the main goals of public sex education.

Ms. Kreinin estimates, however, that in the 1990s, after almost 50 years of sex ed, only about 5 to 10 percent of the sex ed classes in public schools were what she would call "high quality" programs.

In general, she says, there isn't enough interaction in the classroom, and few chances for students to ask the questions they really care about. Teachers have little or no training and often very low comfort levels when it comes to conducting such sessions.

"Kids want to hear about love and values and relationships," she says. "This is not something simply mechanical. it's multidimensional."

Of course this is sensitive territory, something many argue would be best handled at home. But that doesn't appear to be happening in many homes today.

Teens Want Open Dialogue with Parents

"Any public health expert would tell you that the best place to learn about [sex] is at home," says Tina Hoff, vice president of the Kaiser Family Foundation in Menlo Park, Ca. "If this were happening we wouldn't even be having this debate."

Surveys the Kaiser Family Foundation has done of young people show a very strong desire for more information about sex, says Ms. Hoff, and children aged 10 or 11 definitely want that information to come from their parents.

However, if parents don't take advantage of that window of opportunity they may lose it, she adds. Within a few years— about the age of 13 and 14—teens begin to say they prefer talking to their friends. Yet it's a task many parents seem to continue to shirk.

"Survey poll after survey poll shows parents believe that kids should have comprehensive sex ed in school and if you ask them if they should talk to their kids they say yes," Kreinin reports.

But when children are queried, they say they are still waiting to hear from their parents.

A Holistic Approach May Be Best

Some observers are baffled that parents today, who accept prime-time TV shows rife with sexual innuendo, are still so intensely uncomfortable talking about sex with their children.

"We are a sex-saturated and sex-repressed society simultaneously," says Michael Carrera, founder of the Children's Aid Society Carrera Adolescent Pregnancy Prevention Program.

Dr. Carrera believes strongly in the need for what he calls a "holistic" approach to sex education for young people.

He worked for two decades attempting to educate low-income teens about sex in hopes of reasoning them out of irresponsible behavior and teenage pregnancies. But he never felt his message fully got through.

"I finally saw that what I needed to do to get my sexuality message to stick was to deal with all the rest of their lives," he says.

He saw the kids around him using sex in an effort to find power, influence, or love. What they needed, he realized, was not just to learn about the consequences of sex outside marriage, but also to understand all the other avenues to success and self-esteem available to them.

"They needed help with school, jobs, sports, arts, someone to talk to, and someone to talk to about sex," he says.

Statistics Tell the Story

The program Carrera founded now operates nationwide, focusing on mentoring, counseling, job opportunities, companionship, and sex ed for low-income teens.

A recent three-year survey of 12 of its sites showed that students participating had one-third fewer pregnancies and births than teens in a control group.

Yet such success is far from the norm in the US.

According to figures compiled by the Centers for Disease Control and Prevention and the National Campaign to Prevent Teen Pregnancy, in Washington [D.C.], between 10 and

40 percent of US teen girls will get pregnant before the age of 20—double the rate in Britain and 10 times that of the Netherlands.

Some insist there is a link between such statistics and a weak sex ed system.

"Other industrialized nations do a much better job" of giving their young people information about sex, Kreinin says. "They are more comfortable and it is reflected in their kids' behavior."

Despite Progress More Work Is Needed

Yet there is some encouraging news. The number of high school students who say they've never had sexual intercourse rose by almost 10 percent between 1991 and 2001, according to the Centers for Disease Control in Atlanta.

Some speculate that teens today may be reacting against what they perceive to be an overly permissive society. Supporters of abstinence-only programs hope that this could be a sign that their message just might be getting through.

But whatever the cause, say some who work with teens, it doesn't lessen the imperative need to learn to communicate better with young people on this topic.

In society today, "our technology is unbelievable," says Carrera. "But when it comes to talking about sex, we're still antediluvian."

A Sympathetic Ear May Work Best

Sometimes the best way to talk to kids about sex is not to talk about sex at all, some argue. At least not all the time.

"I love this [Carrera's] program because they said, 'Let's not focus on the fact that so many teens have babies and you could be one of them,'" says Nickey-Ann Leon, a junior in college, majoring in communications. "Instead they said, 'Let's focus on the fact that you're intelligent and can do many things with your life.'"

Ms. Leon became involved with the Children's Aid Society Carrera Adolescent Pregnancy Prevention Program in New York when she was 13. She joined, she says, because she wanted to make friends. She hoped a carefully supervised teen group might be one of the few activities her strict parents would approve.

The program changed her life, she says, giving her a chance "to focus on something else, not just on sex."

Frustration Leads to New Approach

Michael Carrera, formerly a professor of health sciences at Hunter College in New York, had educated low-income teens about sex for 20 years and was often praised for his excellent classes.

But he was neither content nor convinced that he was making any progress in reducing teen pregnancy.

"I was in a battle against a tide so powerful I could not make any headway," he says. It occurred to him, however, that the best way to help teens keep sex in its proper context was to ensure that their lives have a broader outlook. To do so, he created a program that focuses on mentoring, finding jobs, counseling, listening—and learning about sex.

As part of the program, sex education combines basic information and practical knowledge about contraceptives with the chance to talk seriously about love and relationships—and why sexual activities are important and require careful thought.

Sex ed at school wasn't effective . . . because it was an uncomfortable setting, where asking a question would have been embarrassing.

Teens Rave About Holistic Program

Sugey Palomares and Melissa Marcial entered the program together in Brooklyn at the age of 13. In a neighborhood where teen pregnancies are the norm, they've bucked the tide and are now both in college.

Their high school provided comprehensive sex ed and yet also offered a nursery because so many students already had babies.

Sex ed at school wasn't effective, the young women say, because it was an uncomfortable setting, where asking a question would have been embarrassing.

At the program, however, they not only had classes but also a counselor they could talk to in private whenever necessary.

"They helped us to understand that you don't have to prove your love to someone by sleeping with him," Ms. Marcial says.

"They were so open with us and let us ask questions about anything," Ms. Palomares adds.

There was also a chance to actually talk to the opposite sex about things like relationships, says Richard Johnson, now a junior in college, who participated at a program site in the Bronx.

"I learned to talk to women, to respect them," Mr. Johnson says. "I just didn't know that before."

Being able to talk about male-female relationships was great, agrees Leon: "It covered emotions and feelings and it wasn't just procedural. It was real."

CHAPTER 4

Are Alternatives to Teen Parenting Good Options?

Chapter Preface

When a teenager finds out she is pregnant, she has several options that range from keeping the baby to choosing adoption to ending her pregnancy through abortion. Of these options, abortion remains the most controversial.

According to the Alan Guttmacher Institute, one-third of all pregnancies of girls aged fifteen to nineteen end in abortion. Like the teen pregnancy rate, the teen abortion rate has been dropping. Abortion has been legal in the United States since 1973, yet many Americans remain conflicted in their views about it. In recent years the political climate has shifted and many states have passed laws restricting access to abortion. For example, as of 2006 thirty-five states had laws that required minors (those under eighteen) to notify their parents before obtaining an abortion. (Some states allow judges to grant waivers in special circumstances.)

Researchers at the City University of New York's Baruch College wondered how the notification laws affected teens. They looked to Texas in studying the issue, choosing the Lone Star State because it is the largest state with a parental notification law and could therefore provide a fair amount of data. The state's law took effect in January 2000. The researchers examined teen abortion records and birth records for the two years before the law took effect (1998–1999) and for three years afterward (2000–2002). The results were reported in the *New England Journal of Medicine* in March 2006.

"The law has definite behavioral effects," lead researcher Ted Joyce told the *Washington Post*. According to his team's analysis, the law caused a dip in the teen abortion rate. The researchers found that in the three years after the law took effect, the abortion rate among fifteen-year-olds was 18 percent lower than it was in the two years before. The abortion rate dropped 25 percent for sixteen-year-olds and 22 percent for seventeen-year-olds. The researchers also noted that second-trimester abortions spiked for girls who became pregnant just prior to their eighteenth birthdays, prompting them to conclude that girls on the cusp of turning eighteen wait to reach that milestone so they can have the procedure without involving their parents.

The results of the Texas study brought mixed reviews. Texas state senator Florence Shapiro told the *Dallas Morning News* that overall, she was pleased with the data. "I strongly believe that the bill we passed accomplished what we were trying to do." Others, including the study's lead researcher, were not so sure. "If this minor did not want to have this birth, is that a good outcome?" Joyce asked. "What are the consequences to the offspring of the women who have the unintended birth?"

The topic of abortion is discussed further in this chapter. Pregnant teens who do not feel ready to become parents sometimes find abortion to be a satisfactory alternative. Others choose adoption. The authors in this chapter look at abortion and adoption and present a variety of viewpoints concerning the pros and cons of these alternatives to teen parenting.

Abortion Is a Good Alternative to Teen Parenting

Children's PressLine

Children's PressLine is a youth media organization that trains children ages eight to eighteen to become journalists with a focus on advocacy for children and their rights. Children's PressLine articles are published in the New York Amsterdam News *and also distributed to hundreds of newspapers across the United States.*

The March for Women's Lives in Washington D.C. [in April 2004 brought] together hundreds of thousands of people to bring attention to abortion rights that, activists say, are being threatened by the current [George W. Bush] administration. [Children's PressLine] spoke to young adults about their firsthand experience with abortion. All interviewees wished to remain anonymous.

Abortion Is a Hard but Reasonable Choice

S.J., 20. We thought we were in love. I was going out with him for about four months when this happened. We weren't using protection. We didn't like how it felt.

Suddenly I became one of the girls my mom always told me to stay away from—the girls me and my friends talk bad about.

We both made the decision [to have the abortion]. We were terrified. I was 16. He was only 20.

We had the abortion two weeks after we found out. When I got to the clinic they told me [that I was] eight weeks [along in the pregnancy].

Children's PressLine, "Teens Grateful for a Second Chance via *Roe v. Wade*," *New York Amsterdam News*, April 22, 2004. p. 18. Reproduced by permission.

What really convinced us [to have the abortion is that] I had no job. I was doing poorly in school or I just didn't go. And my boyfriend's job was only paying $13 an hour.

I got to the clinic around 8:30. The room was packed. There were no seats available and the room wasn't even that big. It was people standing, sitting on the floor. I thought there would be a little more privacy. All the girls looked sick and tired, all holding and leaning on their boyfriends. There had to be like 30 girls: girls my age, women in their 30s, and older women no less than 40. The guys were just sitting there looking into space comforting their girl, holding them, kissing them, whispering useless and unimportant things in their ear.

I was scared. There's four people in the room with you: the doctor, the nurse, the needle man and some other woman. I was so nervous. Obviously, I had sex, but having your stuff wide open and three people staring at it—that's just uncomfortable. Then the needle man stuck me with this big needle. I was screaming. I was so scared. The last thing I remember the doctor was like "shhh," softly.

Now that I look back [on having had an abortion], I couldn't have made a better choice.

An hour later I'm in this other room and this nurse was trying to wake me up. After you can stand they send you off with this big huge [maxi] pad and a lollipop.

It cost $400. My boyfriend paid with his credit card because I was scared that my mom would see the bill. I didn't tell my mom.

Now that I look back, I couldn't have made a better choice. Me and him are not together anymore, and we did not break up on good terms. We don't even speak to each other anymore.

Side Effects of Pregnancy Are Horrible

R.P., 15. [Children's PressLine] spoke with R.P. the day before her 2nd abortion.

I've been sexually active for about a year and a half. I've been pregnant once before, when I was 14. The first time, I just denied it. I took a thousand pregnancy tests just trying to find a negative. When I told my boyfriend, I didn't really know what to feel. I felt really scared and really upset and aggravated with myself and mad at him that he wasn't taking the responsibility he was supposed to take. Last time, I didn't tell my parents, but me and my boyfriend paid for it and got an abortion.

I found out I was pregnant again about a week and a half ago. I freaked out, went home and started crying. I was just upset. I felt stupid. I knew that I either had to have the baby or have an abortion. And I wasn't gonna have the baby. Abortions are painful and emotionally stressful. I felt stupid for not protecting myself for a second time. It just feels better without a condom.

Since he [my boyfriend] smokes a lot of pot, I kinda thought his sperm wasn't really gonna do anything. I thought it was just gone cause he smokes so much, but it was good sperm. [My boyfriend] was there when I took the pregnancy test. I think he was freaked out. I took his virginity and he didn't take mine so the fact that the first girl that he did it with was having a baby, or was pregnant, he got really freaked out—but he was really supportive. He is 18.

I wasn't afraid at all [of statutory rape charges], but he was terrified. He could not stop talking about it. I knew that when I went into the place to get an abortion and to get a sonogram, they wanted him to come [too]. But he didn't wanna come in, "Cause I'll get in trouble for being 18." No one's gonna arrest him. They're gonna care about getting the kid out of me.

[My parents] were upset about it because they knew about my first one and they thought I had been really careless. They're really supportive and they're helping me a lot. I thought [my dad] might be mad, and he is a little mad but not in a grounding kind of way. He's mad but mostly very supportive. My dad knows I smoke pot [and] cigarettes. My dad knows I'm sexually active. Since I just moved out of my mom's house and into my dad's house, she was pissed that I had lied to her about it. I told her that the best way to not get pregnant was abstinence, so she kinda thought I wasn't having sex. She was pissed but still supportive. I'm getting birth control pills. I'm gonna continue being sexually active. I don't know, condoms just really aren't my thing. And I know there's STDs [sexually transmitted diseases] and everything, but if I'm with a boyfriend that I trust and know doesn't have any kind of STDs and I'm on birth control, then I'm not gonna use a condom. I don't want this to happen again. I'm 15 and it's happened twice. That's way too much.

It's gonna be much easier than the last time. First of all, 'cause I told my parents beforehand. Last time I told them after I already got it. The first time I knew I didn't want to have the baby but the thought of something growing inside of me and me just killing it was very upsetting. I was having doubts if I was gonna be able to go through it or not and it was very painful, but I think it will be easier the second time. I have a lot more support this time.

They did teach me sex-ed at school. The information they gave was just not very useful. Like they told us what an abortion was. They didn't tell us the side effects, what it was like afterwards. A guy would have no idea what it was like to go through for a woman's body. Me not liking condoms is my own fault. They taught us to use a condom and I didn't listen, so I don't think they could have done anything.

Being pregnant is just a horrible experience. There are a lot of side effects. I pee every 5 minutes. It's very uncomfortable and aggravating. In school, you can't tell your teachers you're pregnant. You have to go pee the whole entire period 'cause you can go only once a period. I gag every morning.

I want nine babies when I'm older.

Mistakes do happen, and for your whole future to be taken away as your punishment is unreasonable.

Delaying Parenting Keeps Future Bright

D.A., 22. The condom broke. We were going out for three months. She wanted to get rid of it more than I did. We weren't ready anyway because she was getting a full scholarship to college for running and I was getting a full scholarship for basketball. If we had a baby, all that would be ruined.

I was shocked [when I found out she was pregnant]. A whole bunch of [stuff] went through my head. She was mad calm. At first she didn't want to tell me because she knew she couldn't have it. But her friend said she should tell me. She was mad cool, mad reserved. She never let it get to her. I was scared to tell anyone.

I thank God for the people who fought hard to make this legal. I mean, speaking from experience, there is nothing like a second chance. Mistakes do happen, and for your whole future to be taken away as your punishment is unreasonable.

I have a lot going for myself, but I have to focus on myself right now. Don't get me wrong, I want kids, and I want to give them my 100 percent attention and time. But I definitely can't do that right now. So I am very grateful for the choices we have today.

My mom is willing to do anything and everything for me and I would be hurting her if I did something like that to her and to my life.

Adoption Is a Good Alternative to Teen Parenting

Jessica Henman

Jessica Henman teaches childbirth classes at Missouri Baptist Medical Center in St. Louis. She also volunteers her time as a nurse and counselor at the Pregnancy Resource Centers of Greater St. Louis, an organization that provides pregnancy testing, ultrasounds, counseling, medical referrals, and parenting classes to pregnant moms in need.

As educators committed to family-centered maternity care, we recognize that our care is not limited to the birth of a child, but includes the success of the family as a unit and as individuals. In educating teenage mothers and fathers about their choices regarding childbirth and parenting, [many counselors are not] equipped to competently discuss adoption as a viable option. . . . One study showed that 60% of pregnancy counselors did not mention adoption, and of those who did mention it, 40% gave inaccurate information. Perhaps more important is that when accurate adoption information was given, an increase of 19% was seen in adoption plans made. Barriers to adoption include low level of knowledge and lack of support from helping professions, resulting in only 1%–3% of pregnant teens placing their children with adoptive families. . . .

The first, and most vital question for educators to ask is, "Is adoption a healthy choice for teen mothers and fathers and their babies?" This question can be answered both by anecdotal evidence collected from families involved in adoption, as well as from scientific data. . . .

Adoption Yields Positive Outcomes

Scientific evidence for the benefits of adoption to teens and their children comes from a variety of sources. [Studies in the 1980s and 1990s] found that young women who chose adoption for their infants were less likely to rely on welfare, live in poverty, engage in risky sexual behaviors, or have a second baby outside of marriage. They were also likely to attain significantly higher educational levels, get married, and be employed with higher incomes compared to those adolescents who raised a child. It is important to note that, psychologically, mothers who place children in adoptive families frequently acknowledge sadness and feelings of regret over their choice, at times more than mothers who choose to parent; however, when surveyed they were more optimistic, satisfied with their lives, and less likely to be depressed at six months and four years after giving birth than single mothers.

The Robin Hood Foundation found that up to 70% of adolescent mothers are dependent on welfare and 5% of their children are put into foster care later, often "apprehended" by government agencies. Compared to men who become fathers at 20 or 21, adolescent fathers tend to complete one less semester of schooling (often the crucial high school graduating semester), and earn less income over the 18 years following the birth of the child. Fewer than 19% of adolescent mothers wed the fathers of their first children, and nonresident fathers rarely provide financial support to the mother and child. Previous reports that adopted children are much more susceptible to mental health issues have been shown to be biased, ignoring the 95% of adopted persons who are never referred for therapy. Many utilize samples of adolescents who were placed in adoptive homes after spending their early years in an unhealthy home environment. Teens who were adopted as infants are at or above average in many dimensions, including self-esteem, optimism, relationship with parents, school accomplishments, and plans for the future, and do as well as non-adopted children in measures central to mental health. Children of adolescent mothers in the Robin Hood study were in poorer health, were twice as likely to run away from home between the ages of 12 and 16, and were more than two times as likely to be abused or neglected than children of mothers older than 20.

It is estimated that six in ten Americans have 'personal experience' with adoption.

No More Shame

In the past, a shroud of secrecy and disgrace surrounded adoption, incurring shame and emotional trauma of both birth parents and adopted persons. This was perpetuated by inaccurate beliefs, demeaning practices, and criticism by media, health care workers, counselors, and the family members of pregnant women who chose adoption. In the United States, Canada, and other places around the world, adoption law is being refined, cultural barriers are being overcome, and adoption is gaining more and more attention as a way of building healthy families. Adoption has even been hailed as a way to increase tolerance and understanding in the face of changing family structures. It is estimated that six in ten Americans have "personal experience" with adoption, and over 100 million have had adoptions in their immediate family.

In the last several years, laws in at least 18 states and two provinces in Canada have been revised to allow "open adoption," in which the birth parents have some control over the selection of adoptive parents, and have the option of contact with the child after adoption, as agreed upon with the adoptive family. Some of these laws also allow for release of birth records to adult adopted persons who wish to locate their birth parents. The current norm in the United States and Canada (for voluntary adoption placements) is open or semi-open. In the semi-open adoption, contact with birth parents is conducted through an adoption agency, preserving the privacy of all parties involved. This is a change from closed adoptions, in which birth parents and adoptive parents never know each other's identity, and the child may never have any information about his/her biological family. In contrast to past scenarios of babies being whisked away from their mothers at the moment of birth, never to be seen again, the modern birth mother is given options regarding her child's adoption, counseling, financial assistance, and the resources to parent the child should she change her mind. All of this contributes to a greater sense of control and closure for the birth parents. . . .

The most crucial task of parenting . . . is making choices that benefit the child, even if it is painful for the [birth] parent.

Empowerment Is Crucial

[Counselors] may want to have questions prepared to help a pregnant teen and her partner explore their options. Many teens are unprepared psychologically to consider the future consequences of today's decisions. A common expression of pregnant teens is that they have always loved babies, or always wanted to have a baby. Some have not considered the long-term work of parenting, and would benefit from an honest look at what they need to do to prepare for it, whether they consider adoption or not. A few thought-provoking questions could be:

- What are your personal or educational goals in the next five years?

- How much income do you think it takes to raise a baby, a five-year-old, or a ten-year-old? How do you plan to supply that income?

- Who can you count on to support you (financially, emotionally, etc.) in parenting a child?

- What resources do you have to provide childcare while you go to school or work?

- What do you think are the most important ingredients for a healthy family? Can you supply all those ingredients for your child?

- How does the father of this baby plan to be involved in your life and your child's?

- How do you think this child will be affected by your future dating or marriage? How will the child change your future dating or marriage?

- Do you know anyone who was adopted or who has placed a child in an adoptive family? How do they feel about adoption?

- Do you know any women/men who became mothers/fathers as teenagers? How do they feel about parenting?

- Would you be interested in talking with other teens who chose adoption or parenting?

Throughout the decision process, both birth parents should be supported through counseling and encouragement.

The most crucial task of parenting, a task which begins before the birth of the child, is making choices that benefit the child, even if it is painful for the parent. Teens in an unplanned pregnancy need to know that they have a choice to make—whether they have the ability to be effective parents now, or if other, more prepared adults can provide a better life for the child, and potentially for them, as well. We as educators need to have the compassion and the knowledge to be faithful guides as the choice of parenting versus adoption is made. The power to make this choice for themselves is perhaps the most valuable gift we can give young mothers and fathers.

Abortion Has Long-Term, Harmful Effects on Teens

Amy R. Sobie and David C. Reardon

David C. Reardon is director of the Elliot Institute, a nonprofit agency that focuses on research, education, and outreach regarding postabortion issues. Amy R. Sobie has worked at the Elliot Institute and has written many articles for the Post-Abortion Review, *a quarterly publication that explores the impact abortion has on parents, children, and society in general.*

About 20 percent of all abortions taking place in the U.S. are performed on teens. Teenage abortion has been linked to a number of physical and psychological problems, including drug and alcohol abuse, suicide attempts and suicidal ideation [thoughts], and other self-destructive behaviors.

Compared to women who abort at an older age, women who abort as teens are significantly more likely to report more severe emotional injuries related to their abortions. This finding is supported by the fact that women who aborted as teens participate in disproportionately large numbers in post-abortion counseling programs. In the WEBA [Women Exploited by Abortion] study of post-abortive women, for example, more than 40 percent of the women had been teenagers at the time of their abortions.

The Psychological Risks Are Greater for Teens

Compared to women who have abortions in adulthood, teens who abort:

- Are two to four times more likely to commit suicide.

- Are more likely to develop psychological problems.

- Are more likely to have troubled relationships.

- Are generally in need of more counseling and guidance regarding abortion.

- Are nearly three times more likely to be admitted to mental health hospitals than women in general.

Younger women have a more difficult time adjusting to their abortions.

Studies have shown that the major factors in pregnancy decision making among teens are the attitude of the teen's parents, the baby's father, and her peers; the personality of the teen herself; and the cultural and public policy attitudes toward abortion by which she is surrounded. Compared to older women, teens are more likely to abort because of pressure from their parents or sexual partners, putting them at higher risk for adverse psychological effects after abortion.

Teens are also more likely to report having wanted to keep the baby, higher levels of feeling misinformed in pre-abortion counseling, less satisfaction with abortion services and greater post-abortion stress. They consider the abortion procedure itself to be stressful and associated with feelings of guilt, depression and a sense of isolation. Researchers have also found that reports of more severe pain during abortion among younger women are linked to greater levels of anxiety and fear prior to the abortion.

Younger women have a more difficult time adjusting to their abortions. One study found that teenage aborters were more likely to report severe nightmares following abortion and to score higher on scales measuring antisocial traits, paranoia, drug abuse and psychotic delusions than older aborters. Teens were also more likely to use immature coping strategies such as projection of their problems onto others, denial or

"acting out" than older women—strategies researchers speculate might become permanent.

Replacement Pregnancies Are Common

Another study found that less than one fourth of teens were
able to achieve a healthy psychological adaptive process after
their abortions, and many continued to reenact their trauma
through a cycle of repeat pregnancies and abortions. One
study found that on average, 59 percent of teens who had experienced a pregnancy loss—generally due to induced abortion—become pregnant again within 15 months. In another
study, 18 percent of teenage abortion patients had become
pregnant again within two years.

Repeat pregnancies are a symptom of young women "acting out" unresolved abortion issues and the desire to "replace"
the lost pregnancy with another child. Unfortunately, "replace-
ment babies" are often aborted because the woman faces the
same pressures as she did the first time, and sometimes even
more. For example, a New York City study found that teens
who had one previous abortion were four times more likely to
abort their current pregnancy than girls experiencing their
first pregnancy. Another study of teen abortion in Los Angeles
found that 38 percent of the teens had undergone an earlier
abortion and 18 percent had undergone two abortions in the
same year.

Sometimes a teen who has been especially traumatized
will choose abortion as a form of self-punishment or as an
unconscious attempt to resolve her trauma by continually repeating it. In other cases, she may be hoping to continue her
pregnancy but will feel pressured by her parents or partner to
submit to an abortion as "what is best for everyone." In one
heart-wrenching example, a teenage girl reported that she was
forced by her mother to abort four times before she was finally able to insist on keeping her fifth baby.

Teens Face Physical Risks

Teenage abortion patients are up to twice as likely to experience cervical lacerations during abortion compared to older women. This increased risk is thought to be due to the fact that teens have smaller cervixes, which are more difficult to dilate or grasp with instruments.

Teens are also at higher risk for post-abortion infections such as pelvic inflammatory disease (PID) and endometritis (inflammation of the uterus), which may be caused either by the spread of an unrecognized sexually transmitted disease into the uterus during the abortion, or by micro-organisms on the surgical instruments which are inserted into the uterus. Researchers believe that teens may be more susceptible to infections because their bodies are not yet fully developed and do not produce pathogens that are found in the cervical mucus of older women and which can protect them from infection.

Other studies have shown that young women who have had PID previously or who have not had a previous full-term birth are more vulnerable to post-abortion infections. In addition, because teens are less likely than adults to take prescribed antibiotics or follow other regimens for the treatment of medical problems such as infection, they are at greater risk for infertility, hysterectomy, ectopic pregnancy and other serious complications.

Because teens are more likely to abort their first pregnancy, they face other risks as well. For instance, research has shown that an early full term birth can reduce a woman's risk of breast cancer, but that induced abortion of a first pregnancy carries a 30 to 50 percent increased risk of breast cancer. In addition, aborting teens lose the protective effect of having a full-term pregnancy at a younger age, which reduces breast cancer risk.

Late-Term Abortions and Teens

The Centers for Disease Control has reported that 30 percent of teenage abortions occur at or after 13 weeks gestation, compared to only 12 percent of abortions overall. The high rate of late-term abortions among teens is a symptom of how they feel trapped into abortions that they cannot evade.

Women who undergo late-term abortions often delay having the abortion precisely because (1) they have mixed feelings about the decision or feel less satisfied with it, (2) they have religious or moral objections to abortion, or (3) they have a more favorable attitude toward the unborn baby than women who have abortions in the first trimester. Greater ambivalence about abortion increases the likelihood that women will resist advice and pressure from others to abort for a longer period of time, hoping with each passing week that more support for keeping the baby will materialize.

Younger women—especially adolescents—are at significantly higher risk of . . . complications following abortion.

In this regard, polls have consistently found that more teens have pro-life or anti-abortion attitudes than do older women, which may help to explain the much higher late-term abortion rate among teens. No doubt another factor is that teens are more likely to conceal their pregnancies, either out of shame or in an effort to avoid being pressured into an unwanted abortion. After all, many teens know well in advance that their parents or boyfriends will support only one choice: abortion. But teens who conceal their pregnancies are never truly safe from the pressure to abort. Since abortion is legal during all nine months of pregnancy, it's never too late for parents or others to begin pressuring a girl into an abortion once her pregnancy is discovered or revealed.

Late-term abortions, and all of the factors related to ambivalence—such as delay, concealment of the pregnancy, and feeling pressured to abort—are significantly associated with more severe emotional and psychological problems after abortion. Teens who abort in the second and third trimester also face a greater risk of physical complications, including higher rates of endometritis, intrauterine adhesions, PID, cervical incompetence, subsequent miscarriages and ectopic pregnancies, rupture of the uterus and death. In addition, dilation and extraction abortions, frequently used in the second trimester, are associated with low birth weight in later pregnancies, which can cause various health and developmental problems for the baby, including cerebral palsy. . . .

Hazards of Procedure Are Often Overlooked

As shown in this brief review, numerous studies have found that, compared to older women, younger women—especially adolescents—are at significantly higher risk of physical and psychological complications following abortion. But this information is not generally known by the public, and certainly not by the parents who pressure their daughters into abortions.

In many of these cases, the parents truly believe they are helping to protect their daughter's future. They have no idea that they are subjecting her to a physical and psychological trauma that will forever scar her life. Nor will the abortion clinics, who have a vested interest in keeping the dangers of abortion secret, explain the full range of risks to teenagers, their parents, or—in the case of judicial bypass—the judges who stand in the place of the parents.

Abortion is fraught with dangers and risks, especially for younger women who are at greater risk of suffering both physical and psychological complications. The deceptive business practices of abortion clinics—which conceal these risks from these teenaged girls, their parents, and even judges—are nothing less than criminal.

Adoption Has Long-Term, Harmful Effects on Birth Parents

National Adoption Information Clearinghouse

The National Adoption Information Clearinghouse (NAIC) is part of the U.S. Department of Health and Human Services. The NAIC supports programs and legislation that promote the safety, permanency, and well-being of families.

Placing a child for adoption can cause a sense of loss that is all-encompassing. This sense of loss begins with the pregnancy itself as the expectant parents come to accept the reality of the unplanned pregnancy and the loss of their own immediate life plans. Most struggle with the decision to place the child for adoption; those who decide to do so begin to plan for a great loss in their own lives with the hope that placing the child for adoption will result in a better life for their baby and for themselves.

Dealing with Loss Is Difficult

The actual physical separation generally occurs soon after the birth. Many circumstances can have an impact on the birth parents' feelings at the time, including mixed feelings about the adoption placement, support from other family members and the other birth parent, and whether the planned adoption is open (i.e., allowing some later contact with the child). The actions of the agency personnel (if an agency is involved), as well as those of the adoption attorney, adoptive parents, hospital personnel, and physician can all affect the feelings of the birth mother and father as they proceed through the process of the adoption and the termination of their own parental rights.

The birth and the actual surrendering of the baby may prompt feelings of numbness, shock, and denial, as well as grief, in the birth parents. All of these feelings are normal reactions to loss. This particular type of loss is different from a loss through death, however, because there is rarely a public acknowledgment, and friends and family of the birth parents may attempt to ignore the loss by pretending that nothing has happened. In some cases, the secrecy surrounding the pregnancy and adoption may make it difficult for birth parents to seek out and find support as they grieve their loss. In addition, the lack of formal rituals or ceremonies to mark this type of loss may make it more difficult to acknowledge the loss and therefore to acknowledge the grief as a normal process.

When birth parents first deal with their loss, the grief may be expressed as denial. The denial serves as a buffer to shield them from the pain of the loss. This may be followed by sorrow or depression as the loss becomes more real. Anger and guilt may follow, with anger sometimes being directed at those who helped with the adoption placement. The final phases, those of acceptance and resolution, refer not to eliminating the grief permanently but to integrating the loss into ongoing life.

Relationships Become Stressed

Placing a child for adoption may also cause other (secondary) losses, which may add to the grief that birth parents feel. No one fantasizes about having a baby and then giving it up, so expectant parents who are planning to place the child for adoption may grieve for the loss of their parenting roles. They may grieve for the person their child might have become as their son or daughter. These feelings of loss may re-emerge in later years, for instance, [such as] on the child's birthday, or when the child is old enough to start school or to reach other developmental milestones.

Additional losses may occur as a result of the pregnancy and placement. In some cases, the birth mother loses her relationship with the birth father under the stress of the pregnancy, birth, and subsequent placement decision. The birth parents may also lose relationships with their own parents, whose disappointment or disapproval may be accompanied by a lack of support. In extreme cases, the birth mother may need to leave her parents and her home. The birth mother may lose her place in the educational system or in the workplace as a result of the pregnancy. Birth parents may also lose friends who are not supportive of either the pregnancy or the decision to place the child for adoption.

Birth parents may experience guilt and shame for having placed their child for adoption.

Feelings of Guilt and Shame Are Normal

Birth parents may experience guilt and shame for having placed their child for adoption, since societal values reflect a lack of understanding of the circumstances that might prompt birth parents to make an adoption plan for their child. At first, there may be shame associated with the unplanned pregnancy itself and with admitting the situation to parents, friends, co-workers, and others. Shame about the pregnancy may lead to feelings of unworthiness or incompetence about becoming a parent. Once the child is born, the decision to place the child for adoption may prompt new feelings of guilt about "rejecting" the child, no matter how thoughtful the decision. . . .

The shame and guilt felt by birth parents is often supported by the secrecy surrounding the adoption process. Thus, keeping the pregnancy a secret, maintaining secrecy throughout the adoption proceedings, and then treating the experience as unimportant may promote a feeling of shame in birth parents, since the pregnancy and adoption are not even discussed. Birth parents who can discuss their feelings with supportive friends, family members, or professional counselors may more easily come to terms with their decision over time and be able to integrate the experience into their lives.

Placing a child for adoption may trigger identity issues in some birth parents. They may wonder, "Am I a parent?" Some birth parents may experience a sense of incompleteness, because they are parents without a child. Generally, their status as parents is not acknowledged among family and friends. If the birth parents go on to have other children whom they raise, this may also affect how the birth parents view their own identity, as well as that of all their children.

Many birth parents continue to mourn the loss of their child throughout their lifetime.

These questions about identity may also extend to the relationship with the child when the adoption is open. Birth parents who participate in open adoptions may initially wonder how they will fit into that new relationship with their child once the adoptive parents become the legal parents. However, this relationship with the child and adoptive family in an open adoption may evolve so that the birth parents maintain an agreed-upon role in the life of the child. Still, there are few role models for birth parents to help clarify this issue of identity.

Grief May Last a Lifetime

Many birth parents continue to mourn the loss of their child throughout their lifetime, but with varying intensity. For instance, birth parents may continue to track the milestones of their child's life by imagining birthday parties, first days of school, graduation, and more. Some birth parents experience long-standing grief, that is, grief that lasts a very long time and may continue to actually interfere with a birth parent's life many years later. Some of the factors that have been found to be associated with long-standing grief include:

- A birth parent's feeling that she was pressured into placing her child for adoption against her will

- Feelings of guilt and shame regarding the placement

- Lack of opportunity to express feelings about the placement

The personal stories of some birth parents, as well as studies with birth parents in therapy, have indicated that some birth parents experience difficulties beyond long-standing grief. For instance, some birth parents may have trouble forming and maintaining relationships. This may be due to lingering feelings of loss and guilt, or it may be due to a fear of repeating the loss. Other birth parents may attempt to fill the loss quickly by establishing a new relationship, marrying, or giving birth again—without having dealt with the grief of the adoption placement. A few birth parents report being overprotective of their subsequent children, because they are afraid of repeating the experience of separation and loss.

For some birth parents, the ability to establish a successful marriage or long-term relationship may depend on the openness with which they can discuss their past experiences of birth and adoption placement. Some birth parents never tell their spouses or subsequent children of their earlier child. Others are comfortable enough with their decision to be able to share their past.

Acceptance of the loss and working through the grief does not mean that birth parents forget their birth child and never again feel sorrow or regret for the loss. Rather, it means that they are able to move forward with their lives and to integrate this loss into their ongoing lives. For those in an open adoption, this may mean developing a new relationship with the child and the adoptive parents. For birth parents whose child was adopted in a closed adoption, it may mean learning to live with uncertainty about whether the parent will ever see the child again. . . .

While the birth parent will never forget the child, it is important that the birth parent adapts to the new circumstances and comes to terms with any regret. When birth parents are able to integrate the loss into their lives and gain some feeling of control, they can then move on to deal with whatever else life presents to them.

CHAPTER 5

Should Society View Teen Parenting Favorably?

Chapter Preface

For decades school systems have struggled with how to handle pregnant teens. Before the 1972 passage of Title IX legislation, many pregnant teens were dismissed from school under a "when you show, you go" policy. While Title IX is best known for the benefits it brings females concerning equal access to sports, its guarantee of educational equity has helped pregnant teens as well.

Since the passage of the legislation schools have not been allowed to dismiss pregnant teens. Many, however, are sent off to alternative schools—away from the general population of students. Some educational policy experts question whether these institutions are adequate in providing girls with an appropriate education on which to build future success.

One researcher studying the education of pregnant teens is Wanda Pillow, an associate professor of educational policy studies at the University of Illinois at Champaign-Urbana. She is also the author of *Unfit Subjects: Educational Policy and the Teen Mother*. Over the course of her career Pillow has interviewed countless pregnant teens about their experiences in school settings. Many complained that they were written up for tardiness or absences related to their pregnancy or child care and that they could not eat or use the restroom as often as they needed. Others lamented that they had to squeeze themselves into small desk seats. In her book Pillow writes that she observed the seating problem so many times that "it just became this visual for me of how we are still sending a clear message to the pregnant teen that she does not fit within the school, she does not fit within education."

Pillow reports that the presence of pregnant teens in schools causes struggles within most communities because many people still have an underlying belief that the presence of a pregnant teen will cause the spread of sexual promiscuity to others. In addition, Pillow believes that despite all of the support programs that have been implemented to help pregnant and parenting teens, schools overall continue to shortchange this population. She also laments that there is no specific policy spelling out what rights pregnant teens have in the school setting. "Presently, beyond forbidding expulsion, there is no case law to enforce or guide the provision of educational services for teen mothers at the local or state level." Just as school administrators have struggled with the issue of teen pregnancy and parenting, society at large continues its debate on how to handle the matter. In this chapter the authors consider whether society should view teen parenting favorably.

Teen Pregnancy and Teen Parenting Are Biologically Normal

Frederica Mathewes-Green

A regular contributor to National Review Online, *Frederica Mathewes-Green also writes for National Public Radio's* Morning Edition, Christianity Today, *and Beliefnet.com. She is the author of the book* Gender: Men, Women, Sex and Feminism.

True Love Waits. Wait Training. Worth Waiting For. The slogans of teen abstinence programs reveal a basic fact of human nature: teens, sex, and waiting aren't a natural combination.

Over the last 50 years the wait has gotten longer. In 1950, the average first-time bride was just over 20; in 1998 she was five years older, and her husband was pushing 27. If that June groom had launched into puberty at 12, he'd been waiting more than half his life.

If he *had* been waiting, that is. Sex is the sugar coating on the drive to reproduce, and that drive is nearly overwhelming. It's supposed to be; it's the survival engine of the human race. Fighting it means fighting a basic bodily instinct, akin to fighting thirst.

Yet despite the conflict between liberals and conservatives on nearly every topic available, this is one point on which they firmly agree: Young people absolutely must not have children. Though they disagree on means—conservatives advocate abstinence, liberals favor contraception—they shake hands on that common goal. The younger generation must not produce a younger generation.

Early Parenting Has Benefits

But teen pregnancy, in itself, is not such a bad thing. By the age of 18, a young woman's body is well prepared for child-bearing. Young men are equally qualified to do their part. Both may have better success at the enterprise than they would in later years, as some health risks—Cesarean section and Down Syndrome, for example—increase with passing years. (The dangers we associate with teen pregnancy, on the other hand, are behavioral, not biological: drug use, STD's [sexually transmitted diseases], prior abortion, extreme youth, and lack of prenatal care.) A woman's fertility has already begun to decline at 25—one reason the population-control crowd promotes delayed childbearing. Early childbearing also rewards a woman's health with added protection against breast cancer.

Humans are designed to reproduce in their teens, and they're potentially very good at it.

Younger moms and dads are likely to be more nimble at child-rearing as well, less apt to be exhausted by toddlers' perpetual motion, less creaky-in-the-joints when it's time to swing from the monkey bars. I suspect that younger parents will also be more patient with boys-will-be-boys rambunction, and less likely than weary 40-somethings to beg pediatricians for drugs to control supposed pathology. Humans are designed to reproduce in their teens, and they're potentially very good at it. That's why they want to so much.

Teen pregnancy is not the problem. *Unwed* teen pregnancy is the problem. It's childbearing outside marriage that causes all the trouble. Restore an environment that supports younger marriage, and you won't have to fight biology for a decade or more.

Teen Marriage and Sex Used to Be Normal

Most of us blanch at the thought of our children marrying under the age of 25, much less under 20. The immediate reaction is: "They're too immature." We expect teenagers to be self-centered and impulsive, incapable of shouldering the responsibilities of adulthood. But it wasn't always that way; through much of history, teen marriage and childbearing was the norm. Most of us would find our family trees dotted with many teen marriages.

Of course, those were the days when grown teens were presumed to be truly "young adults." It's hard for us to imagine such a thing today. It's not that young people are inherently incapable of responsibility—history disproves that—but that we no longer expect it. Only a few decades ago a high-school diploma was taken as proof of adulthood, or at least as a promise that the skinny kid holding it was ready to start acting like one. Many a boy went from graduation to a world of daily labor that he would not leave until he was gray: many a girl began turning a corner of a small apartment into a nursery. Expectations may have been humble, but they were achievable, and many good families were formed this way.

It's odd that kids thought to be too irresponsible for marriage are expected instead to practice heroic abstinence or diligent contraception.

Hidden in that scenario is an unstated presumption, that a young adult can earn enough to support a family. Over the course of history, the age of marriage has generally been bounded by puberty on the one hand, and the ability to support a family on the other. In good times, folks marry young; when prospects are poor, couples struggle and save toward their wedding day. A culture where men don't marry until 27 would normally feature elements like repeated crop failures or economic depression.

That's not the case in America today. Instead we have an *artificial* situation which causes marriage to be delayed. The age that a man, or woman, can earn a reasonable income has been steadily increasing as education has been dumbed down. The condition of basic employability that used to be demonstrated by a high-school diploma now requires a bachelor's degree, and professional careers that used to be accessible with a bachelor's now require a master's degree or more. Years keep passing while kids keep trying to attain the credentials that adult earning requires.

Financial ability isn't our only concern, however; we're convinced that young people are simply incapable of adult responsibility. We expect that they will have poor control of their impulses, be self-centered and emotional, and be incapable of visualizing consequences. (It's odd that kids thought to be too irresponsible for marriage are expected instead to practice heroic abstinence or diligent contraception.) The assumption of teen irresponsibility has broader roots than just our estimation of the nature of adolescence; it involves our very idea of the purpose of childhood.

Society Should Support Early Unions

Until a century or so ago, it was presumed that children were in training to be adults. From early years children helped keep the house or tend the family business or farm, assuming more responsibility each day. By late teens, children were ready to graduate to full adulthood, a status they received as an honor. How early this transition might begin is indicated by the number of traditional religious and social coming-of-age ceremonies that are administered at ages as young as 12 or 13.

But we no longer think of children as adults-in-progress. Childhood is no longer a training ground but a playground, and because we love our children and feel nostalgia for our own childhoods, we want them to be able to linger there as long as possible. We cultivate the idea of idyllic, carefree childhood, and as the years for education have stretched so have the bounds of that playground, so that we expect even "kids" in their mid-to-late twenties to avoid settling down. Again, it's not that people that age *couldn't* be responsible; their ancestors were. It's that anyone, offered a chance to kick back and play, will generally seize the opportunity. If our culture assumed that 50-year-olds would take a year-long break from responsibility, have all their expenses paid by someone else, spend their time having fun and making forgivable mistakes, our malls would be overrun by middle-aged delinquents.

But don't young marriages tend to end in divorce? If we communicate to young people that we think they're inherently incompetent, that will become a self-fulfilling prophecy, but it was not always the case. In fact, in the days when people married younger, divorce was much rarer. During the last half of the 20th century, as brides' age rose from 20 to 25, the divorce rate doubled. The trend toward older, and presumptively more mature, couples didn't result in stronger marriages. Marital durability has more to do with the expectations and support of surrounding society than with the partners' age.

A pattern of late marriage may actually *increase* the rate of divorce. During that initial decade of physical adulthood, young people may not be getting married, but they're still falling in love. They fall in love, and break up, and undergo terrible pain, but find that with time they get over it. They may do this many times. Gradually, they get used to it; they learn that they can give their hearts away, and take them back again; they learn to shield their hearts from access in the first place. They learn to approach a relationship with the goal of getting what they want, and keep their bags packed by the door. By the time they marry they may have had many opportunities to learn how to walk away from a promise. They've been training for divorce.

Delaying Sex Is Unrealistic

As we know too well, a social pattern of delayed marriage doesn't mean delayed sex. In 1950, there were 14 births per thousand unmarried women; in 1998, the rate had leapt to 44. Even that astounding increase doesn't tell the whole story. In 1950 the numbers of births generally corresponded to the numbers of pregnancies, but by 1998 we must add in many more unwed pregnancies that didn't come to birth, but ended in abortion, as roughly one in four of all pregnancies do. My home city of Baltimore wins the blue ribbon for out-of-wedlock childbearing: in 2001, 77 percent of all births were to unwed mothers.

There are a number of interlocking reasons for this rise in unwed childbearing, but one factor must surely be that when the requirements presumed necessary for marriage rise too high, some people simply parachute out. It's one thing to ask fidgety kids to abstain until they finish high school at 18. When the expectation instead is to wait until 25 or 27, many will decline to wait at all. We're saddened, but no longer surprised, at girls having babies at the age of 12 or 13. Between 1940 and 1998, the rate at which girls 10–14 had their first babies almost doubled. These young moms' sexual experiences are usually classified as "non-voluntary" or "not wanted." Asking boys to wait until marriage is one way a healthy culture protects young girls.

The idea of returning to an era of young marriage still seems daunting, for good reason. It is not just a matter of tying the knot between dreamy-eyed 18-year-olds and tossing them out into world. Our ancestors were able to marry young because they were surrounded by a network of support enabling that step. Young people are not intrinsically incompetent, but they do still have lots of learning to do, just like newlyweds of any age. In generations past a young couple would be surrounded by family and friends who could guide and support them, not just in navigating the shoals of new marriage, but also in the practical skills of making a family work, keeping a budget, repairing a leaky roof, changing a leaky diaper.

It is not good for man to be alone; it's not good for a young couple to be isolated, either. In this era of extended education, couples who marry young will likely do so before finishing college, and that will require some sacrifices. They can't expect to "have it all." Of the three factors—living on their own, having babies, and both partners going to school full-time—something is going to have to give. But young marriage can succeed, as it always has, with the support of family and friends.

Early Childbearing Can Be Rewarding

I got married a week after college graduation, and both my husband and I immediately went to graduate school. We made ends meet by working as janitors in the evenings, mopping floors and cleaning toilets. We were far from home, but our church was our home, and through the kindness of more-experienced families we had many kinds of support—in fact, all that we needed. When our first child was born we were so flooded with diapers, clothes, and gifts that our only expense was the hospital bill.

Our daughter and older son also married and started families young. Things don't come easy for those who buck the norm, but with the help of family, church, and creative college-to-work programs, both young families are making their way. Early marriage can't happen in a vacuum; it requires support from many directions, and it would be foolish to pretend the costs aren't high.

The rewards are high as well. It is wonderful to see our son and daughter blooming in strong, joyful marriages, and an unexpected joy to count a new daughter and son in our family circle. Our cup overflows with grandchildren as well: . . . We have four grandbabies, though the oldest is barely two. I'm 49.

It's interesting to think about the future. What if the oldest grandbaby also marries young, and has his first child at the age of 20? I would hold my great-grandchild at 67. There could even follow a great-great-grand at 87. I will go into old age far from lonely. My children and their children would be grown up then too, and available to surround the younger generations with many resourceful minds and loving hearts. Even more outrageous things are possible: I come from a long-lived family, some of whom went on past the age of 100. How large a family might I live to see?

Such speculation becomes dizzying—yet these daydreams are not impossible, and surely not unprecedented. Closely looped, mutually supporting generations must have been a common sight, in older days when young marriage was affirmed, and young people were allowed to do what comes naturally.

Teen Mothers Can Be Responsible Members of Society

Marilyn Gardner

Marilyn Gardner is a staff writer for the Christian Science Monitor.

Jennifer Lind was 18 and the president of her senior class when a little plastic square in a home pregnancy test turned pink, changing her life forever. It confirmed her suspicions that she was pregnant.

Goodbye, college plans. Hello, brave new world of teenage motherhood.

Officials at her school stripped her of her post as class president on grounds that she was not an appropriate role model. A guidance counselor told her she would never be able to go to college. "I believed him," recalls Ms. Lind, of Peterborough, N.H. Even her parents turned their backs on her until several months after her son, Jonathan, was born.

Yet Lind, like many other young women in her situation, is proving the skeptics and naysayers wrong. She is one of 35 teenage mothers, all of them now adults, who share their trials and triumphs in *You Look Too Young to Be a Mom*, a new anthology edited by Deborah Davis. By giving teen mothers a rare chance to speak for themselves, Ms. Davis hopes to break a long-standing silence and challenge negative stereotypes.

Teen Moms Are Still Stigmatized

In 2002, 425,000 babies were born to teenage mothers. That represents a 30 percent decline since 1991—a drop that reflects lower rates for all births. Experts also attribute it to less teenage sex and more contraception.

Marilyn Gardner, "They Change Diapers and Perceptions," *Christian Science Monitor*, May 19, 2004, p. 11. Copyright © 2004 The Christian Science Publishing Society. All rights reserved. Reproduced by permission from *Christian Science Monitor* (www.csmonitor.com).

Yet despite greater acceptance in some circles, these young mothers find that the scarlet letter still exists. In their case, the A stands for adolescent pregnancy.

"Many young moms comment about the dirty looks they get in supermarkets and on the street," Ms. Davis says. Their parents are often hurt and angry. Teachers may doubt their chances for success. Even doctors and nurses are sometimes less patient with teens in labor than they are with other women during childbirth, Davis finds.

When she solicited essays from teenage mothers across the United States and Canada, she received nearly 200 submissions from girls in all economic backgrounds. A majority were white, mirroring the fact that most teen mothers in the US are Caucasian. Latinas and blacks also sent stories. Almost all graduated from high school, and some have gone on to college.

Success Is a Long and Hard Journey

No one pretends the journey has been easy.

"I went from being a strong, intelligent class president to having nobody around," Lind says, explaining her initial anger and bitterness [after her pregnancy became known]. She never had a baby shower. That first year after their son was born, her husband even forgot to wish her a happy Mother's Day.

"I realized I needed to take control," she says. "The only one who could make our situation better was me. I needed to forgive my parents and to get my parents to forgive me. Once I learned to forgive the world for the prejudice against young moms, I was able to say, You know what, I'm not a bad person."

Today Lind's son is 8, and she has a 4-year-old daughter, Divorced, she has held a patchwork of jobs to support her children, ranging from data analyst and real estate agent to waitress, art model, and landscape gardener. She is also studying for a bachelor's degree in health science. Lind and her mother now enjoy a close relationship, and she and her father are "a lot closer than we were." But, she adds, "it's been a long road to get there."

Finding Stability Is Possible

For Samantha Lucas, the long road began when she was a high school junior. Like other teens expecting babies, she was saddened by her friends' lack of support. "You say 'pregnant' when you're 17 and they gasp," says Mrs. Lucas, of Easley, S.C. "It's like you tell someone there's a fire. After that first second of shock, they're gone."

With her dreams of going to art school in New York and being a "single independent girl" dashed, Lucas and her boyfriend—now her husband—settled into youthful domesticity with the birth of their daughter.

"After about two weeks of having her home, it all fell in place for me," she says. Now she and her husband are approaching their seventh wedding anniversary. She works at home as a medical transcriptionist and is attending college part time.

Still, despite her success and stability, Lucas sometimes envies her unencumbered contemporaries. "There are days when I'd just love to hang out with a friend, and not think about buying groceries or paying the mortgage," she says. "I still wake up and say, Oh my gosh, I can't believe I'm doing this. It's so hard."

Attending College Is Possible

Hard is also the word Jackie Lanni uses to describe her foray into motherhood at 18. Determined to succeed on her own, she refused to accept welfare or food stamps following the birth of her son.

Instead, after attending high school classes every day, she hurried to two part-time jobs. She felt "obligated to do it the hard way, so no one could point an accusing finger at me."

Although many young women share Ms. Lanni's reluctance to rely on public assistance, nearly 80 percent of unmarried teen mothers receive welfare at some point, according to the National Campaign to Prevent Teen Pregnancy. In 2001, the monthly cash payment to families receiving Temporary Assistance to Needy Families averaged $288 for one child and $362 for two children.

"For single mothers in general, you have only two choices—take a handout forever or take a handout for a while," says Elizabeth Slater of Toronto, whose daughter was born [in 2001] when she was 19. "You have to have an education to support a child."

One common thread running through the richly colored tapestry of these women's lives is a determination to defy stereotypes that portray young mothers as lazy, dependent, and irresponsible.

But getting an education means surmounting many obstacles, from a lack of money and time to a lack of student housing for single parents. Katherine Arnoldi of New York, once a teenage mother herself, is writing a book about how the top 300 colleges and universities in the US accommodate single parents. She calls her findings "dismal." Many schools require freshmen to live on campus but provide no on-campus housing for families.

"The top schools are the worst offenders," says Ms. Arnoldi, author of *The Amazing True Story of a Single Teenage Mom*. She finds large state schools to be the best, offering more housing and more day care. Pointing to other bright spots, she lauds the University of California, Davis, for accepting vouchers for federally subsidized housing. And Indiana State University at Bloomington has a sorority for single mothers.

Determination Plays a Key Role

Latisha Boyd, who grew up in a housing project in the Bronx, gave birth to a son when she was 19. For the first six months, she and her baby were homeless, bouncing from one relative's home to another. Finally, her son's great-aunt helped her to get an apartment.

She began attending church, and her renewed faith helped to turn her life around. Eventually, Ms. Boyd received a master's degree from Adelphi University. She is a social worker in Maryland.

One common thread running through the richly colored tapestry of these women's lives is a determination to defy stereotypes that portray young mothers as lazy, dependent, and irresponsible.

Some mothers receive emotional or financial support from their parents. Others credit mentors and sympathetic employers. Slowly, success has come, one day, one feeding, one diaper change, one paycheck, one college course at a time. In the process, recrimination and doubt gradually give way to growing confidence.

Whatever challenges teen parents face, Davis says, their situation doesn't have to be a disaster.

"Studies show that while young mothers have a hard time in the first years, they do come through it. There's a limited period of time when things are rough, but most teen mothers and their children turn out fine."

Ms. Lanni, whose son is now 10, looks forward to graduating from law school at the University of Arizona. Summing up the challenge of young parenthood, she says, "Being a teenage mom is like being a woman in corporate America. You have to work twice as hard to get half the credit."

Society Should Condemn Teen Parenting

Chuck Muth

Chuck Muth is president of the nonprofit Citizen Outreach, a Washington, D.C.–based public policy advocacy group whose mission is to reduce and limit the powers of the government. Muth is a regular contributor to the Federal Observer, *a right-wing national newspaper.*

[Syndicated columnist] Larry Elder penned a rather disturbing column [in late 2004]. He noted that, "According to the *World Almanac* 2005, nearly 70 percent of black children are born outside of wedlock." And children born into such circumstances, not surprisingly, end up having a *lot* more problems than kids born into a married household. Go figure.

Teen Motherhood Is Dishonorable

The first thing that occurred to me upon reading this was that unless a bunch of white men were going around raping and impregnating black women, then this is one problem the black community simply cannot blame on "whitey." Physician, heal thyself.

But this problem is even deeper. It's about a serious, un-American entitlement mind set taking hold in this country, and not just among minorities.

Elder writes specifically about Fantasia Barrino, winner of the . . . *American Idol* contest [in 2004]; an unmarried mother who "dropped out of school in ninth grade, got pregnant and gave birth at age 17." Obviously, she's not alone in choosing this dangerous path at such a young age. What's troubling is that girls such as Fantasia think this is something to be proud

Chuck Muth, "Muth: American Idle—the New American Dream," *The Federal Observer Online*, January 3, 2005. Reproduced by permission of the author.

of. Indeed, in a song titled "Baby Mama" on her recently released CD, Fantasia refers to single-parent motherhood as "a badge of honor."

Honor? What's "honorable" about irresponsibly getting yourself knocked up and bringing a baby into the world when you have no husband, no job and no education? Your baby gets to start life with two strikes against him while standing blindfolded at the plate with a whiffle-ball bat on his shoulder against [pitching legend] Nolan Ryan. Gee, what an honor.

Entitlement Mentality Seems Pervasive

But it's even worse. Get this line from the song: "I see you get that support check in the mail, Ya open and you're like, 'What the hell.' You say, 'This ain't even half of day care.' Sayin' to yourself, 'This here ain't fair.' To all my girls who don't get no help. Who gotta do everything by yourself . . ."

It's hard to know where to begin here, although the fact that Fantasia ain't got no good English tends to confirm the notion that she, indeed, dropped out of school *way* too early.

I'm assuming, and not without reason, that the "support check" Fantasia refers to is from Uncle Sam and not the baby's father. That a large segment of the American population continues to be dependent upon the government in this post–welfare reform world means we still have a long way to go.

But think about what Fantasia laments with regard to the paucity of her government check. That it won't cover the cost of food? Clothing? A roof over her head? Medical care? No. That it doesn't cover even half the cost of paying someone else to raise *her* child during the day. Fantasia apparently believes that being an absentee parent is not only a good thing, but an entitlement as well. She plays, you pay.

"This here ain't fair," huh?

Early Pregnancy Leads to Government Dependency

Apparently no one ever told Fantasia that life AIN'T fair. Get over it. There are no guarantees in life ... even in America. You're not even "entitled" to happiness. All our Founders provided for was a God-given right to PURSUE happiness, not attain it. Some do. Some don't. It might not be "fair." But that's life. Get used to it. And stop whining.

Finally, the kicker: "To all my girls who don't get no help. Who gotta do everything by yourself."

"Who don't get no help"? Certainly not in the grammar department, but I digress.

What help and from whom does Fantasia think "her girls" are entitled? From the kid's no-account father? OK, sure. But now for the Million Dollar Question: Did Fantasia's girls stop, for even a moment, to think about that *before* climbing into the sack with the bums who "don't give them no help" now? Or did they stop to think, "Hey, maybe I should get on the pill first"? Yeah, sure they did.

These poor girls have to do everything by themselves, huh? Well, they sure made the decision to do the horizontal bop unprotected by themselves. They didn't consult you and I in advance to see if we *wanted* to pay for the consequences of their actions. Why in the world should *we* pay after the fact for *their* choice?

That this is the kind of un-American, government-dependent thinking which wins awards on *American Idol* is all I need to know to be grateful that I've never watched the show. *American Idol*, my eye. There's nothing to idolize here. *American Idle* would be more like it.

The Lives of Teen Mothers Are Hard and Stressful

Jan Farrington

Jan Farrington writes about a variety of issues for Current Health 2, *a publication of the Weekly Reader Corporation. The publication, which provides news and analysis of general health and fitness issues, is aimed at children in grades seven through twelve.*

The realities of teen parenting: Reality? Check out what it means to have a child while you're just barely out of childhood yourself.

On the one hand, few teen parents are likely to experience the holiday-card sweetness of the movie *Where the Heart Is*, in which abandoned teen Novalee Nation has her baby in a Wal-Mart closed for the night. Quick plot summary: She's adopted by the whole town and sheltered by a strong older woman (who dies and leaves her money!), works her way toward a career as a photographer, builds a house, and finds a smart, caring guy to love and marry.

And on the other hand? It's the image of teen parenthood as a hopeless situation: a grim story of poverty and lost dreams, of being "trapped" in a life you never wanted. Yes, many teen parents have it very rough, and too many don't seem able to create a happy, stable life for themselves and their children. That's a reality. But there also are teen parents facing their challenges and working hard to beat the odds.

Nope, the reality is that there is no one-story-fits-all version of "how it is" to be a teen parent. Just ask Elizabeth, who has seen things "work out" for some teens—and go very badly for others. We talked to her recently about her life since the day when she discovered she was going to have a baby

Jan Farrington, "The Realities of Teen Parenting," *Current Health 2*, vol. 29, no. 7 supplement, March 2003, p. 1. Reproduced by permission.

News Upsets Parents

"It was the night before I was supposed to have surgery on my shoulder," Elizabeth remembers. "I was 15, a sophomore. The hospital had been doing a lot of routine tests, and then a couple of nurses came in and said 'You can't go in for surgery. You're pregnant.' They were really nice about it. My dad got very quiet. He didn't look angry—just really, really sad."

Elizabeth is a tall, slim girl with glossy dark hair and a quiet, calm manner. She is 18 now, and 2-year-old Hannah is demanding all her attention. This morning, Mom isn't at school or at work, so Hannah wants it all: a fresh bowl of cereal, a drink, a toy, a ride on Mommy's hip . . . and all her attention.

"The first thing that shocked my parents was finding out that I was having sex at all," says Elizabeth. She had been dating since she was 13, and the guy she was seeing at the time was 19 years old. "I was never the problem kid in our family. But before I found out I was pregnant, it was a really low point for me. I was very depressed about relationships and family issues that were piling up, even thinking about suicide.

"And it's funny—I didn't intend to get pregnant. But when I found out, I felt almost relieved, almost happy. Somebody was going to need me. It gave my life a new focus."

Pregnancy Is Shocking to Peers

Elizabeth's parents talked about sending her to live with a grandparent in another state, and about giving the baby up for adoption. From the beginning, though, Elizabeth was determined to keep the baby. Her parents didn't want her to tell anyone, and worried about what would happen when she began to "show" at school.

"Once I got looking around, I noticed a lot of girls at school who were pregnant," says Elizabeth. "I started showing by my fourth month, and people I knew were kind of shocked. They said I didn't seem like the kind of girl who would have a baby so soon."

Elizabeth says she never thought about leaving school. "I knew school was very, very important." Elizabeth had plans, and she didn't want to give them up. She talked with her counselor, who referred her to a social worker for the school district. Together, they agreed that she would begin her junior year at the district's "New Lives" program for teen parents. At New Lives, teen moms (and dads, too, though Elizabeth says she never saw any "guy" students) had on-site day care for their babies, and could keep up with assignments sent from their home schools—until they were ready to return to a regular campus.

Fights with Family Are Common

Meanwhile, Elizabeth was "getting huge."

"My dad was still saying that if I was going to keep the baby, I would have to move out and pay my own bills," Elizabeth recalls.

We had a lot of fights [after the baby was born] . . . because I thought my mom was trying to take over.

"But he was the one who made sure I walked every night, and when Hannah was born, you could see he was such a proud grandpa. She had jaundice, so he would take her out in the sunshine and talk to her. They were real buddies."

Elizabeth went on living at home, and returned to her old high school early in her junior year. She took a full load of courses and worked part-time while her own mother stayed at home with baby Hannah. She was surrounded by family and friends—even though at times she fought with her mother about who was going to be Hannah's "real" mom.

Financial problems and emotional stress are two issues teen mothers face on a regular basis. Getty Images.

"We had a lot of fights back then because I thought my mom was trying to take over, and I've seen kids before who grew up calling their grandma 'Mom.' I didn't want that—so when Hannah was colicky, I would sit up with her all night. When I went to work part-time at a fabric shop, the first thing I bought there was a pink fleece blanket for Hannah, because it was important to me that I give her things. She still loves that blanket."

Support Networks Prove Beneficial

When Elizabeth graduated, her family and friends let her know how proud they were of her—and Elizabeth understands how much difference their support has made in helping her to stay in school and become a good mother.

"There was a lot of support around me. A lot of girls who don't have that kind of situation just don't stay in school," she says. "I met girls at New Lives who automatically married their baby's father, and it often caused lots of problems. And I've seen quite a few of the girls who went through the program with me have another baby, which really complicates their lives."

Elizabeth is taking college classes at a nearby campus, and trying to decide whether she wants to be a neonatal nurse (for newborn babies) or an elementary school teacher. Most of the people she meets, she says, think she's in her mid-20s. "I do feel old for my age. I don't have much time for a social life—but really, I never did."

The baby is not the problem. . . . It's all the other things— the emotional stress, the money problems.

She says that Hannah's father, now 22, is still "a player" who likes to date much younger girls. "I think he somehow just knows how to pick the right girls," she says with a little shrug. "He tried for a long time to get me to do stuff I didn't want to do, and I always said no. But then finally, he caught me at a very low time, and I just gave in."

Having a Baby Alters Life Plans

"If I were talking to somebody younger about all this, I think I'd want to make sure they know that having the baby is not the bad part. The baby is not the problem. I love Hannah so much. But it's all the other things—the emotional stress, the money problems, and I know I'm still rebuilding the trust people used to have in me, especially my parents. I think you need to talk to kids when they're 11 or 12, before they've already settled on what they're going to do, and tell them: It's better to wait, to just not do it."

Elizabeth is beating the odds. She's finished high school, is doing well in college, and has made some great plans for the future. But it hasn't been easy, and Elizabeth says every single day is a juggling act.

"Every day is set to a certain beat," says Elizabeth. "And if anything changes, it all gets out of whack—like if I'm called to fill in for someone at work suddenly." Elizabeth's situation with Hannah is very dependent on her parents' willingness to commit a lot of time and energy to helping her raise the baby. Many teens don't have that kind of support.

It's really, really hard. I've got to get up with him during the night, then get up early for school.

Will Elizabeth see her plans through to the end and become a teacher or nurse? She's very determined. But getting pregnant at age 15 wasn't what she had planned for her life, and there's no denying that becoming a mom has changed her expectations for herself—and made everything she does much harder to achieve.

"A few years ago, Elizabeth was absolutely sure she wanted to go to medical school and become a pediatrician," her mom says, shaking her head. "Now, she can't see spending all that time away from Hannah. She's had to give up lots of dreams."

Reality Can Be Overwhelming

Our teen mom Elizabeth has had a rough time. But in some ways, she's one of the lucky ones—because she has a network of family and friends around to help and support her. Most teen parents, however, find the day-to-day grind of parenting a pretty hard way to live.

The National Campaign to Prevent Teen Pregnancy (NCPTP), a Washington, D.C.–based group, collected quotes from teen parents for their Web site, www.teenpregnancy.org.

Here's what teens around the country are saying about their experience of becoming teen parents:

- It's really, really hard. I've got to get up with him during the night, then get up early for school. My mother watches the baby during the day. But in the evening, I've got to do my homework, feed him, give him a bath, get him to sleep, and get myself ready for the next day.

- After the baby was born, I called the father and said, "You have a son." He was like, "No, I don't. You have a son."

- I got pregnant a month before my 17th birthday. My son's father and I got married five months ago, and we're already separated. I live in an emergency shelter for teen moms. . . . I've only been out once without him. The rest of the time, he goes everywhere with me. I only get four hours of sleep a night. I miss my friends. I don't see them anymore because they have their own lives.

- Changing their diapers and feeding them, and bathing them, and playing with them. It's not like you can just say, "OK, I'm tired of being a father," and just give up. That child's still here.

Organizations to Contact

Advocates for Youth
2000 M St. NW, Suite 750, Washington, DC   20036
(202) 419-3420 • fax: (202) 419-1448
e-mail: info@advocatesforyouth.org
Web site: www.advocatesforyouth.org

Advocates for Youth creates programs for and advocates for policies that help adolescents make informed and responsible decisions about their reproductive and sexual health. Specifically, the group works toward improving access to reproductive health care and promotes the development of school-based clinics. It publishes numerous advocacy kits, including the five-volume *Communities Responding to the Challenge of Adolescent Pregnancy Prevention*, as well as pamphlets with such topics as *An Emergency Option for Preventing Pregnancy After Sex* and *America's Least Wanted: Sexually Transmitted Diseases*. Many publications are available in Spanish.

Aim for Success
PO Box 550336, Dallas, TX   75355
(972) 422-2322
Web site: www.aimforsuccess.org

Aim for Success is an educational organization that teaches abstinence through programs that promote self-control, self-respect, and self-discipline, believing these skills will help teens resist sexual pressure. Aim for Success is the largest provider of abstinence education programs in the United States. It publishes the bimonthly newsletter *Tips on Encouraging Sexual Abstinence* as well as a book and audio series titled *Teens, Sex, and Choices*.

Alan Guttmacher Institute (AGI)
120 Wall St., 21st Floor., New York, NY   10005

(212) 248-1111 • fax: (212) 248-1951
e-mail: info@guttmacher.org
Web site: www.guttmacher.org

AGI's mission is to protect and broaden the reproductive choices available to both men and women in the United States and around the world. The nonprofit organization works to develop effective family planning and sex education programs through policy analysis, public education, and sexual and reproductive health research. Among its publications are various reports, including *Adding It Up: The Benefits of Investing in Sexual and Reproductive Health Care* and *Into a New World: Young Women's Sexual and Reproductive Lives*. It also publishes the compilation *Readings on Teenagers and Sex Education*.

American Social Health Association (ASHA)
PO Box 13827, Research Triangle Park, NC 27709
(919) 361-8400 • fax: (919) 361-8425
e-mail: info@ashastd.org
Web site: www.ashastd.org

ASHA is dedicated to improving the health of individuals, families, and their communities by working to stop the spread of sexually transmitted diseases (STDs). The organization provides both public and college health clinics with informational brochures and books that explain the risks and transmission of STDs, as well as information about prevention, testing, and treatment. The group bills itself as "America's authority for sexually transmitted disease information." A portion of its Web site is devoted to teen sexual health. It publishes the *State of the Nation Report 2005: Challenges Facing STD Prevention in Youth*, as well as the brochures *Condoms, Contraceptives, and STDs* and *Teens & STDs*.

Concerned Women for America (CWA)
1015 Fifteenth St. NW, Suite 1100, Washington, DC 20005
(202) 488-7000 • fax: (202) 488-0806
Web site: www.cwfa.org

CWA is one of the nation's largest public policy women's organizations. Its mission is to bring public policy into alignment with biblical principles and values. CWA works toward this goal by lobbying Congress to pass laws aimed at strengthening the traditional nuclear family. It strongly opposes abortion and premarital sex. CWA produces several brochures, including *What Your Teacher Didn't Tell You About Abstinence* and *Why Children Need Fathers: Five Critical Trends*.

Family Research Council (FRC)
801 G St. NW, Washington, DC   20001
(202) 393-2100 • fax: (202) 393-2134
Web site: www.frc.org

With a mission of "defending family, faith, and freedom," the council seeks to influence and formulate public policy that strengthens and promotes the traditional family. The FRC, a research, resource, and educational organization, supports public policies that promote the Judeo-Christian worldview. Among its publications are the papers *Why Wait: The Benefits of Abstinence Until Marriage, Talking Points on Abstinence Until Marriage Education*, and *Room for More Virtue*.

Healthy Teen Network
509 Second St. NE, Washington, DC   20002
(202) 547-8814 • fax: (202) 547-8815
e-mail: healthyteens@healthyteennetwork.org
Web site: www.healthyteennetwork.org

Formerly known as the National Organization on Adolescent Pregnancy, Parenting and Prevention, the Healthy Teen Network is a national membership organization comprising practitioners, policy makers, and state and local coalitions concerned with the struggles of pregnant and parenting adolescents. The group believes that adolescents will make responsible decisions about their reproductive health and sexuality if given complete, accurate, and culturally relevant information, skills, resources, and support. It publishes *Pregnancy Basics* magazine as well as the report *Another Chance: Preventing Additional Births to Teen Mothers*.

Heritage Foundation

214 Massachusetts Ave. NE, Washington, DC   20002-4999
(202) 546-4400 • fax: (202) 546-8328
e-mail: info@heritage.org
Web site: www.heritage.org

This research and educational think tank promotes conservative public policies based on the principles of free enterprise, limited government, individual freedom, traditional American values, and a strong national defense. The Heritage Foundation believes that illegitimacy and teen pregnancy are caused in part by the welfare system, which, the foundation believes, helps perpetuate the problem. Each year, the foundation publishes about ten books and 250 research reports, including *Teenage Sexual Abstinence and Academic Achievement, Adolescent Virginity Pledges, Condom Use, and Sexually Transmitted Diseases Among Young Adults,* and *Sexually Active Teenagers Are More Likely to Be Depressed and to Attempt Suicide.*

National Campaign to Prevent Teen Pregnancy

1776 Massachusetts Ave. NW, Suite 200
Washington, DC   20036
(202) 478-8500 • (202) 478-8588
e-mail: campaign@teenpregnancy.org
Web site: www.teenpregnancy.org

The nonprofit, nonpartisan National Campaign to Prevent Teen Pregnancy seeks to improve the well-being of the nation's children, youth, and families by reducing the teen pregnancy rate. It does this by promoting education and policies aimed at urging teens to adopt values, activities, and actions consistent with a pregnancy-free adolescence. Among its publications are opinion polls, pamphlets, and reports, including *14 & Younger: The Sexual Behavior of Young Adolescents, Do Abstinence-Only Programs Delay the Initiation of Sex Among Young People and Reduce Teen Pregnancy?* and *A Good Time: After-School Programs to Reduce Teen Pregnancy.*

National Institute of Child Health and Human Development (NICHD)

PO Box 3006, Rockville, MD   20847
(800) 370-2943 • fax: (301) 984-1473
e-mail: nichdinformationresourcecenter@mail.nih.gov
Web site: www.nichd.nih.gov

As part of the National Institutes of Health, the NICHD works to ensure that babies are born healthy and that women are protected from the harmful effects sometimes associated with reproduction. The NICHD promotes policies aimed at helping children achieve their full potential for healthy and productive lives. Its publications include the reports *Today's Issues No. 10: Declining Teen Birth Rates* and *America's Children: Key National Indicators of Well-Being, 2005.*

Planned Parenthood Federation of America

434 W. Thirty-third St., New York, NY   10001
(212) 541-7800 • fax: (212) 245-1845
e-mail: communications@ppfa.org
Web site: www.plannedparenthood.org

Planned Parenthood believes women have a fundamental right to manage their fertility regardless of their income, marital status, race, ethnicity, sexual orientation, age, national origin, or residence. The organization pushes for governmental policies that guarantee these rights and ensure access to reproductive health services. It provides comprehensive reproductive and complementary health care services in communities across the United States. Among its publications is the report *Abstinence-Only 'Sex' Education and Adolescent Sexuality*, as well as the fact sheets "Laws Requiring Parental Consent or Notification for Minors' Abortion" and "Reducing Teenage Pregnancy." Many are available in Spanish.

Sexuality Information and Education Council of the U.S. (SIECUS)

130 W. Forty-second St., Suite 350
New York, NY   10036-7802

(212) 819-9770 • fax: (212) 819-9776
e-mail: siecus@siecus.org
Web site: www.siecus.org

Composed of educators, physicians, and social workers, SIECUS believes that all people, including adolescents, have the right to access information on sexuality. The group encourages responsible sexual behavior by promoting comprehensive sex education that includes information on AIDS and STDs, instruction on contraceptives and their use, and discussions on homosexuality. SIECUS publishes fact sheets and in-depth reports, including *But Does It Work? Improving Evaluations of Sexuality Education*, *The Politics of Sexuality Education*, and *Young People Talk About Sex*. It also produces *Families Are Talking*, a newsletter that includes information to guide parents and caregivers in discussing sexuality with their children.

Bibliography

Books

Joyce C. Abma — *Teenagers in the United States: Sexual Activity, Contraceptive Use, and Childbearing, 2002.* Hyattsville, MD: U.S. Department of Health and Human Services, Centers for Disease Control and Prevention, National Center for Health Statistics, 2004.

John Bancroft, ed. — *Sexual Development in Childhood.* Bloomington: Indiana University Press, 2003.

John G. Borkowski, Deborah A. Keogh, Keri Weed, and Thomas L. Whitman — *Interwoven Lives: Adolescent Mothers and Their Children.* Mahwah, NJ: Lawrence Erlbaum Associates, 2001.

Vicki Burns — *The Experience of Having Become Sexually Active for Adolescent Mothers.* Columbia: University of Missouri, 2003.

Leon Dash — *When Children Want Children: The Urban Crisis of Teenage Childbearing.* Chicago: University of Illinois Press, 2003.

Naomi Farber — *Adolescent Pregnancy: Policy and Prevention Services.* New York: Springer, 2003.

Janice M. Irvine — *Talk About Sex: The Battles over Sex Education in the United States.* Berkeley and Los Angeles: University of California Press, 2002.

Bonnie J. Ross Leadbeater and Niobe Way — *Growing Up Fast: Transitions to Early Adulthood of Inner-City Adolescent Mothers.* Mahwah, NJ: Lawrence Erlbaum Associates, 2001.

Judith Levine — *Harmful to Minors: The Perils of Protecting Children from Sex.* New York: Thunder's Mouth, 2003.

Wendy Luttrell — *Pregnant Bodies, Fertile Minds: Race, Gender, and the Schooling of Pregnant Teens.* New York: Routledge, 2003.

Elizabeth Merrick — *Reconceiving Black Adolescent Childbearing.* Boulder, CO: Westview, 2001.

Adam Pertman — *Adoption Nation: How the Adoption Revolution Is Transforming America.* New York: Basic Books, 2001.

Wanda S. Pillow — *Unfit Subjects: Educational Policy and the Teen Mother.* New York: RoutledgeFalmer, 2004.

Beatrice Sparks, ed. — *Annie's Baby: The Diary of Anonymous, a Pregnant Teenager.* New York: Avon, 2005.

Deborah L. Tolman — *Dilemmas of Desire: Teenage Girls Talk About Sexuality.* Cambridge, MA: Harvard University Press, 2005.

Sabrina Weil	*The Real Truth About Teens and Sex.* New York: Penguin, 2005.
Dorrie Williams-Wheeler	*The Unplanned Pregnancy Book for Teens and College Students.* Virginia Beach, VA: Sparkledoll, 2004.
Franklin E. Zimring	*An American Travesty: Legal Responses to Adolescent Sexual Offending.* Chicago: University of Chicago Press, 2004.

Periodicals

Matt Apuzzo	"Pledging Virginity No Shield for STD's," *Houston Chronicle*, March 19, 2005.
John Barry	"The Term of Teen Pregnancy," *St. Petersburg (FL) Times*, June 8, 2002.
Nina Bernstein	"Behind Fall in Pregnancy, a New Teenage Culture of Restraint," *New York Times*, March 7, 2004.
Kathryn Chinn	"Kids Getting Mixed Messages on Sex," *Denver Post*, August 28, 2005.
Ceci Connolly	"As Teen Pregnancy Dropped, So Did Child Poverty; Study Looks at Decline over 10-Year Period," *Washington Post*, April 14, 2005.
Ceci Connolly	"Some Abstinence Programs Mislead Teens, Report Says," *Washington Post*, December 2, 2004.

Bruce Cook — "Teens' Abstinence from Sex Rarely 'Backfires,'" *Atlanta Journal-Constitution*, April 18, 2005.

Theodore Dalrymple — "A Nation of Paedophiles; If Sex with Children Is So Wicked, Why Are We Relaxed About Under-Age Pregnancy?" *New Statesman*, August 9, 2004.

Julianna Deardorff, Nancy A. Gonzales, Scott Christopher, Mark W. Roosa, and Roger E. Milsap — "Early Puberty and Adolescent Pregnancy: The Influence of Alcohol Use," *Pediatrics*, December 2005.

Willa M. Doswell, Malick Kouyate, and Jerome Taylor — "The Role of Spirituality Preventing Early Sexual Behavior," *American Journal of Health Studies*, 2003.

Mary Dykeman and Cindy Gray — "Zero Adolescent Pregnancy: A Prevention Program at Work That Works," *International Childbirth Education Association*, June 2005.

Frank Greve — "U.S. Teen Pregnancy Rate Falls," *Pittsburgh Post-Gazette*, October 2, 2005.

Albert R. Hunt — "Beware the Moral Cops," *Wall Street Journal*, December 2, 2004.

Sharon Jayson — "Teens Define Sex in New Ways: Shocked Parents Don't Understand Casual Attitude," *USA Today*, October 19, 2005.

Tracy Johnson	"'My Life Is Ruined,'" *Campus Life*, November 2000.
Katy Kelly	"Just Don't Do It! Are We Teaching Our Kids Way Too Much About Sex? Or Not Nearly Enough?" *U.S. News & World Report*, October 17, 2005.
Karen MacPherson	"Experts Worry Childhood Is Over-sexed," *Pittsburgh Post-Gazette*, May 8, 2005.
Anne Mulrine	"Risky Business: Teens Are Having More Sex—and Getting More Diseases. But Is Telling Them to Wait the Answer?" *U.S News & World Report*, May 27, 2002.
Alison Overholt	"Mommyhood Before Marriage," *Cosmopolitan*, October 2005.
Philadelphia Inquirer	"Study: Condoms Don't Boost Teen Sex," May 29, 2003.
Angela Phillips	"It Is Time We Adults Grew Up: We Now Know That Comprehensive Sex Education Cuts Teenage Pregnancy Rates. It Should Be Compulsory," *Guardian* (Manchester, UK), July 1, 2005.
Joyce Howard Price	"Half of New Unwed Mothers in Poverty," *Washington Times*, October 14, 2005.

Janet Reeves "Research, into Practice: Young Fathers Are Generally Depicted as Feckless. However, Recent Research Highlights Their Desire to Be Good Parents," *Community Care*, May 20, 2004.

Ellen Ruby-Markie "Teen Motherhood: Shared Burden," *Memphis Commercial Appeal*, May 7, 2003.

Jan Schakowsky "Q: Do Parents Always Have a Right to Know When Their Teen Is Seeking Birth Control? No: Forcing Parental Notification Will Lead to Deadly Illegal Abortions and Higher Rates of Teen Pregnancy," *Insight on the News*, October 29, 2002.

Mark Townsend "Violence Blamed on Teenage Mums: Study Claims That Immature Young Parents with Poor Discipline Techniques Are Creating Aggressive Children," *London Observer*, October 16, 2005.

Women's Health Weekly "Adolescent Health: Teenage Pregnancy May Put Girls at Risk for Osteoporosis," January 8, 2004.

Index